Interactions and Screens in Research and Education

Christine Develotte, Amélie Bouquain,
Tatiana Codreanu, Christelle Combe,
Morgane Domanchin,
Mabrouka El Hachani, Dorothée Furnon,
Jean-François Grassin, Samira Ibnelkaïd,
Justine Lascar, Joséphine Rémon,
Caroline Vincent

Ateliers [sens public]

Les Ateliers de [sens public] - 11/2023 - Montreal
Collective fablab and fabulous collective, les Ateliers are a ship that
sails in the Sens public archipelago, with the support of the Canada
Research Chair in Digital Textualities and the Centre de recherche
interuniversitaire sur les humanités numériques.

Cover : Hélène Beauchef

Legal deposit : 2023, 4th quarter
Library and Archives Canada
Bibliothèque et Archives nationales du Québec

An expanded version of this manuscript is available in open access
on ateliers.sens-public.org.

This book is a translation of *Fabrique de l'interaction parmi les écrans*,
published in June 2021 by les Ateliers de [sens public].

ISBN :
978-2-924925-22-5 (print)
978-2-924925-24-9 (EPUB)
978-2-924925-23-2 (PDF)
978-2-924925-25-6 (HTML)

/[

Table des matières

Introduction

Christine Develotte

The volume *Interactions and Screens in Research and Education* presents a self-reflexive research project that was conducted in and on a doctoral seminar focused on Multimodal Screen Interactions (or IMPEC as per the French acronym). This introduction is written in the first person as it tries to elucidate the choices I made as director of this seminar[1]. It aims to specify the goals, the genesis and the theoretical and practical grounding of research that was conducted as a collective project under my leadership[2].

The two main goals of this research are related to the specific nature of the digital environment on which and in which we work :

— The analysis of a concrete research training seminar that was both face-to-face (on site in Lyon) and remote (via a videoconferencing platform and telepresence robots), leading to a reconceptualisation of interactions related to experience in a hybrid context.

— The positioning of this study in favour of open science that forms part of the digital humanities and new scholarly formats that are currently being developed. Ultimately, the data gathered will thus be available to the scientific community and the results will be published in different forms, digital forms in particular.

---

1. Given the collegial mode of functioning that will be explained further on, first person singular and plural will be used alternately in this introduction.

2. This "Digital Presences" research project has benefitted from the financial support of the ASLAN Labex since 2018.

The context of research on Screen-based Multimodal Interactions (IMPEC : *Interactions Multimodales Par ECran*)

I will start by describing the research context surrounding this volume : both the prior or concomitant studies that inspired the volume, and how it is situated in the continuity of my own work.

Multidisciplinary inspirations

Undoubtedly as a result of my own multidisciplinary academic background [3], the sources of inspiration for my research are not restricted to a single domain. I provide four examples here that have had the greatest influence on this project.

Mauro Carbone (philosophy)

Mauro Carbone and his *"Vivre par(mi) les écrans"* research group have been examining how we live with screens from a phenomenological perspective since 2013. He posits that screens, which today are the habitual interface for our relationships to the world, to others and even to ourselves, produce "regimes of visibility" (Carbone, Dalmasso, and Bodini 2018, 23).

In our situation of communication combining screens of different sizes in artefacts [4] or as part of a platform, the *premediation* of the presence of remote participants is clearly

---

3. I began by studying literature, then psychology and sociology, and then applied linguistics, combined with a period of research in communication sciences.

4. The notion of "artefact" designates any non-animated object without specifying its function. For more information, check "Theoretical and methodological framework for visual reflexive ethology", section "Remote communication artefacts and their positions in the room".

apparent. Participants are not featured in the same way depending on the screens that broadcast their presence. As Francesco Casetti (2018, 53) reminds us :

> The screen only becomes a screen from the point of view of the device with which it is associated, and which links it to the set of practices that produce it as such.

And because different telepresence screens are associated with specific affordances, they permit certain possibilities of expression or not : for example, participants using the Adobe Connect platform can express themselves in chats, whereas participants using robots cannot. We can thus agree with Carbone when he says that "a certain 'regime of visibility' is intertwined with a certain 'regime of sayability' by virtue of directing the attention and inattention both of our gaze and of our discourse" (Carbone, Dalmasso, and Bodini 2018, 25).

One of the goals of our research is to show which ethos and discourse are associated with each screen. Reciprocally we aim to study how the participants in-situ address remote participants depending (or not) on the different screens mediating their presence.

Louise Merzeau (information and communication sciences)

Louise Merzeau calls the advent of digital technology an "environmental transformation that affects structures and relationships … [and that] calls into question the conceptual models that serve to formalise them" (Merzeau 2009, 23). This calling into question of conceptual models is also needed when considering exchanges via screens (video-conferencing or telepresence robots). This is the point of view adopted in my earlier work (Develotte, Kern, and Lamy 2011; Kern and Develotte 2018) and one of the crucial goals of this project is to propose conceptual innovations based on multidisciplinary analyses [5] of the data gathered.

Susan Herring and Marie-Anne Paveau (linguistics)

In 1996, Susan Herring [6] launched the field of linguistic research on "computer-mediated communication" (1996).
She provides a new synthetic schema of multimodal interactive communication that goes from email, via the telepresence robot, to the 3D immersive platform avatar (Herring 2015).
Like Susan Herring, French linguist Marie-Anne Paveau has mainly studied written digital discourse. She presents her work as "a response to the need to invent new concepts, tools and limits to describe how forms of discourse native to the internet function from a qualitative and ecological perspective". Paveau defines "discourse native to the internet" as "the set of all verbal productions that are elaborated online, regardless of the devices, interfaces, platforms or writing tools used" (Paveau 2017, 8). She posits that "native digital language productions" (2017, 8) involve a non-human dimension (machine, software, algorithm...) that informs and shapes what can be said (2017, 11).
This conceptualisation of digital discourse is embodied in the expression "discursive technology".
The anteposition in French of the term "technology" (*technologie discursive*) underscores the paramount importance of this dimension in discourse that is indelibly marked by it. This is what we will describe in this volume : the manner of

---

5. Check "Theoretical and methodological framework for visual reflexive ethology".

6. As a leading figure in linguistic studies of online communication, Herring was the editor-in-chief of the journal *Computer-Mediated Communication* from 2004 to 2007 and then of the journal *Language@Internet*.

speaking and interacting with remote participants is unique and depends on the specificities and affordances of each artefact.

Gregory Bateson (anthropology of communication)

There is nothing new about having a multidisciplinary team study a common corpus. This adventure was undertaken in *The Natural History of an Interview* (McQuown 1971) recounted by Wendy Leeds-Hurwitz [7] (1988). I will discuss some of the elements of this work below as well as its connections to the present project.

This multidisciplinary project [8] that would represent a turning point in research in social communication was launched in 1955-1956 at the Center for Advanced Study in the Behavioral Sciences at Stanford University.

From this pioneering project in communication, I chose not to define a prior theoretical orientation [9], to respect the ecology of interactions and to open up the data to a multidisciplinary team of researchers. This project also taught the importance of setting a precise research schedule from the start and involving all the members of the group. Bateson, who was the only researcher present in the film, was in fact very uneasy about having his postural, mimetic and gestural behaviour dissected on screen by his colleagues. In our project, all the participants were involved in the same

---

7. Leeds-Hurwitz's study was discussed in greater detail in one of the first presentations of our research during the seminar on "*Méthodes Pour La Recherche Autour De La Communication Multimodale 'Artéfactée'*" (meaning : As seen from the perspective of the IMPEC seminar : Methodological Choices for Reflexive Research).

8. Which initially brought together two psychiatrists, two linguists and three anthropologists.

9. I suggested that the general research framework be based on the naturalistic approach developed by Jacques Cosnier under the heading of "comprehensive ethology".

undertaking, took the same risks (in terms of their image) and made the same commitments.

My research on screen-based interaction

I began to work on screen-based interaction in 2002, usually in educational contexts, before turning to synchronous online conversation starting in 2006.

Describing online conversation

The research project entitled *Décrire la conversation* ("Describing conversation"; Cosnier, Kerbrat-Orecchioni, and Bouchard (1987)) was inspired by *The Natural History of an Interview*, and in 2006, as a next logical step, I invited my colleagues to join me in co-editing the volume entitled *Décrire la conversation en ligne* ("Describing online conversation"; Develotte, Kern, and Lamy (2011)).

In this volume, using a common corpus given to different researchers to study, we were able to show that desktop videoconferencing communication had revisited the principles revealed for face-to-face conversation. Interactional synchrony, for example, cannot be separated from the quality of the digital flow and from distortion of the audio or video signal, which induces a necessary adjustment on behalf of the speakers.

Directly following up on *Décrire la conversation en ligne*, the aim here will be to understand how this polylogical situation changes participants' behaviour in comparison to the dialogical situation studied earlier. The second aim will be to analyse the effect of the simultaneous use of various means of communication.

Ethical dimensions of the research

Filming interlocutors inevitably leads to the problem of accessing "natural" data.

We believe self-reflexive research [10] to be closer to "natural" data rather than "elicited" data. In our case, even if having the ultimate goal of studying interactive behaviour could potentially influence participants' behaviour, the doctoral seminar held a genuine educational function of training doctoral students.

Promoting open science

In *Décrire la conversation en ligne*, the video data we used to study online conversations were then included in the CLAPI database [11] which was developed by the ICAR laboratory and is accessible to all researchers [12]. Today, ten years later, as open science has become more widely accepted, we naturally adopted the prospect of sharing the data associated with our project.

Moreover, an encounter with Marcello Vitali-Rosati in 2018 gave shape to the idea of publishing our results in digital form – an idea which we intuitively had thought about, but which we did not know already existed. This immediately seemed the best way to exploit the multimodal nature of our video data [13].

The IMPEC research group

The IMPEC group is a working group that was formed in 2013 based on researchers' shared interest in screen-based interactions. The group is committed to a multidisciplinary approach, mainly involving applied linguistics, cognitive

---

10. Check "Theoretical and methodological framework for visual reflexive ethology".

11. *Corpus de Langue Parlée en Interaction* (Corpus of Spoken Language in Interaction).

12. Interactions, Corpus, Apprentissages, Représentations (Interaction, Corpus, Learning, Representations).

13. Check "Theoretical and methodological framework for visual reflexive ethology".

sciences, and communication sciences. The group studies a variety of situations, both individual (i.e., telephone, video games, etc.) and collective (the use of screens in face-to-face or remote contexts, such as talks, webinars, network games, or museum visits). These situations can occur within a professional setting with computer screens, specific screens (control screens), and in various private contexts, and may involve the general public or a particular audience (i.e., children, young adults, seniors). These situations are usually multimodal in a broad sense; in other words, they connect the multimodality that emerges between people (verbal, paraverbal and non-verbal) and the multimodality present in any type of content (i.e., text, audio, still and moving images) visible on screens.

The group organises its work around a biennial conference and a seminar which I coordinate [14].

The hybrid IMPEC seminar

The aim of this monthly seminar is to provide scientific support to the doctoral students I supervise. The seminars help to stimulate the students' critical thinking by involving guest researchers, in addition to providing the students with the opportunity to present their ongoing work. The majority of the doctoral students involved were pursuing thesis topics connected to digital communication, usually in the context of education. Since some students lived too far away to attend the seminars physically, we started using videoconferencing with a computer placed in the middle of the table in the seminar room. Although this improvised system did allow participants to attend remotely, it was not very convenient. The participants in-situ had to remember to move the computer so that the webcam was always poin-

---

14. The videos both of the conferences and of the seminar are freely available on the IMPEC website.

ting in the right direction for the remote participants, and the latter sometimes found themselves looking at a whiteboard or in some other insignificant direction.

From videoconferencing to the "Digital presence" project

In 2016, we tried both to improve the technical set-up and to involve the set-up in the construction of a corpus suitable for studying different aspects of screen-based interactions, which had been the focus of the seminar from the start.
The initial idea was thus to continue to host remote participants using various types of devices or artefacts in order to analyse the effects of the different autonomy of the artefacts on the dynamics of the seminar.

The polyartefacted doctoral seminar

Here, I will present the project participants and the characteristics of the seminar. A more precise description of the tools of communication and their affordances will be provided in the chapter "Theoretical and methodological framework for visual reflexive ethology".

Participants

16 people participated in the research project on some level or another, with varying degrees of involvement at different times. The group was mixed from several points of view : it was international and each of its members had a different level of competency in using the artefacts (ranging from no experience to mastery). The team was intergenerational and included three disciplines ; the prevalence of applied linguistics refers to my home discipline and to the nine participants scientifically related to me (i.e students, doctoral students, or former doctoral students). This is an important element as these links that were established over several years prior to the project form the basis for a socioemotional stability of relationships within the group. Mo-

reover, I knew the "external" colleagues who were invited to join the team, since I had already collaborated with them.

Characteristics of the seminar

Since the seminar is dedicated to doctoral students, I attach great importance to the working atmosphere so that younger participants feel comfortable expressing themselves [15]. Benevolence is a word that I often use and that I try as much as possible to put into practice. For me it is essential that any question can be asked and all points of view can be expressed without anyone having to fear being judged by the other participants. The adopted policy on the dynamics of exchanges also led me to limit my own speaking time and to express myself more concisely to provide more time for doctoral students and less experienced participants.

In addition, I tried to conduct the research project so as to provide the doctoral students with a scientific experience as part of their doctoral training. In that perspective, the doctoral students were involved in a research project that was not exactly their own, but they could draw inspiration from the project's theories and methodologies. This seminar thus links training FOR research to involvement IN research, fostering a form of teaching based on lived experience [16]. The seminar also attempts to apply the concept of Zone of Proximal Development (Vygotski 1985) by involving colleagues of different academic ranks in different exchanges.

---

15. I myself attended doctoral seminars as a doctoral student in which only senior researchers spoke and I never dared to intervene. Here, I tried to do the opposite by creating a space for congenial exchanges.

16. This view echoes with the projects that I previously developed in language didactics for teaching a language by way of interpersonal exchanges among students (Develotte 2008).

Finally, we prioritised the idea of developing what Richard Kern and I have called a "nurturing matrix" (Kern and Develotte 2018, 9) : a matrix that encourages collaboration among participants. Ensuring that all the participants were involved in the scholarly adventure in which I had invited them to take part was one of the main motivations for fostering collaboration in the different stages of our research : during the seminar, during the development of the research project, and during the process of writing this book [17].

Work programme

I planned a work schedule spread out over four years in response to my painful past experience of collective research projects that were inordinately extended in time and that ended up exhausting the interest and energy of the researchers. The four-year duration required us to adopt an intense rhythm, which was sometimes a little difficult to maintain. Nevertheless, the variety of the tasks in our timetable held participants' interest and maintained their involvement. Moreover, as our research topic has been evolving very rapidly due to improvements in technical means, the objective was also to reduce the time separating the group's lived experience and making the research results available to the scholarly community. Finally, the above-mentioned encounter with Marcello Vitali Rosati, which was decisive for the editorial choices made for this work, allowed us to demarcate the different phases of the proposed schedule.

Choice of chapters

The writing of the different chapters in this book took place in two stages, which are reflected in the two-part presenta-

---

17. Check "Theoretical and methodological framework for visual reflexive ethology".

tion below. First, we present three thematic chapters covering aspects that initially seemed to be the most salient for the purposes of our research; then three other intersecting chapters, which often draw on the results of the previous chapters.

Dimensions involved in polyartefacted situations.

The three aspects that were chosen at the outset are attention, corporeality and politeness.

Jean-François Grassin, Mabrouka El Hachani, Joséphine Rémon and Caroline Vincent wrote the first chapter entitled "Attentional affordances in an instrumented seminar". This chapter examines how attention is reconceived within the seminar in question as a dual attentional set-up, in its material construction of space and in its relational construction. The analysis focuses on sequences of the co-construction of attention within the specific horizon of expectation of the seminar, which is itself modified by the technological set-up.

The second chapter, written by Samira Ibnelkaïd and Dorothée Furnon, considers the technobodily modalities of enacting intersubjectivity and reveals that participants structure their perception and action through different states of mediation : "demediation", "remediation" and "immediation". Participants manage these states of mediation by embodying specific roles in the interactions, such as "procurators", "witnesses" and "sentinels" through distributed agency. The latter gives rise to phenomena of reification of the animate and of personification of the artefact, leading to the enactment of an artifacted intercorporeality.

The third chapter by Amélie Bouquain, Tatiana Codreanu and Christelle Combe deals with politeness using the microsociological theories of Erving Goffman (1974) and the analysis of online conversation (Develotte, Kern, and Lamy 2011). It revisits these notions, which are simultaneously linguistic, transsemiotic and cultural, and reveals new norms of politeness in the context of artefacted interactions.

The diachronic evolution of experience

The second part of the volume undertakes a review of the dimensions of the polyartefacted seminar that take on meaning experientially over time.

The chapter "Autonomy and artefactual presence in a polyartefacted seminar", written by Amélie Bouquain, Christelle Combe and Joséphine Rémon, analyses the effects of presence via a comparative study of the potentialities of telepresence systems. Depending on the interactional co-construction undertaken by the participants, effects of presence of devices define an artefactual or an interactional presence around issues of autonomy of movement, visual and sound ajustement, stealthy presence and forced presence.

Samira Ibnelkaïd and Caroline Vincent examine "Digital bugs and interactional failures in the service of a collective intelligence". This chapter is based on the analytical results of the thematic chapters, which are related to a semantic study of the final assessment questionnaires. The chapter reveals the co-construction of a form of collective intelligence and the enacting of a group ethos that does not necessarily reduce situations of technical bugs but instead reinforces a feeling of personal efficacy (Bandura 1980) in the individual and collective capacities of remediation.

Finally, Morgane Domanchin, Mabrouka El Hachani and Jean-François Grassin consider the polyartefacted doctoral seminar and its potential for research training. This last chapter regards the seminar as a space of doctoral training and, more precisely, the construction of the ethos of four doctoral students based on identifying the traces of their investment during the different phases of the seminar. Moments of collaborative learning are classified by way of a visual schema illustrating the potential acquisition of technical and scholarly competencies. The aim of the chapter is to uncover the dimensions that doctoral training promotes : notably, the socio-emotional, artefactual and international dimensions that enhance the experience of young researchers and the support we provide them.

To conclude this introduction, I would like to note that the research covered in this volume is both modest and ambitious. The research is modest in that it focuses on a limited duration (six months) and involves only a dozen people within a given educational situation. But our project is ambitious by virtue of its openness : our research seeks to provide theoretical justification for a multidisciplinary approach to an object of research, a particular digital ecosystem. Based on the analyses that have been carried out, our project proposes new concepts that are suited to the realities and experiences described, to these situated "discursive technologies". Our project also aims to contribute to the free and open dissemination of knowledge by way of the online publication of our results and by making the data freely available to the scholarly community.

Our research project constitutes both the culmination of a professional trajectory and the starting point for a multidisciplinary toolkit of digital interactions.

References

Bandura, Albert. 1980. *L'apprentissage Social*. Bruxelles : P. Mardaga.

Carbone, Mauro, Anna Caterina Dalmasso, and Jacopo Bodini. 2018. *Des Pouvoirs Des Écrans*. Sesto San Giovanni : Mimesis. Online.

Casetti, Francesco. 2018. "Sur Le Statut de l'écran." In *Des Pouvoirs Des Écrans*, 53–67. Sesto San Giovanni : Mimesis. Online.

Cosnier, Jacques, Catherine Kerbrat-Orecchioni, and Robert Bouchard. 1987. *Décrire La Conversation*. Lyon :
Presses universitaires de Lyon. Online.

Develotte, Christine. 2008. "Approche de l'autonomie
Dans Un Dispositif En Ligne : Le Cas Du Dispositif Le
Français En (Première) Ligne." *Revue Japonaise de Didac-
tique Du Français* 3 (1) : 37–56. Online.

Develotte, Christine, Richard Kern, and Marie-Noëlle
Lamy, eds. 2011. *Décrire La Conversation En Ligne : La
Face à Face Distanciel*. Lyon : ENS Éditions.

Goffman, Erving. 1974. *Les Rites d'interaction*. Paris : Les Éditions de Minuit. Online.

Herring, Susan C. 1996. *Computer-Mediated Communication*.
John Benjamins Publishing Company. Online.

———. 2015. "New Frontiers in Interactive Multimodal
Communication." In *The Routledge Handbook of Language
and Digital Communication*, edited by Alexandra Geor-
gakopoulou and Tereza Spilioti, 398–402. Routledge
Handbooks in Applied Linguistics. London : Routledge. Online.

Kern, Richard, and Christine Develotte. 2018. *Screens and
Scenes : Multimodal Communication in Online Intercultural
Encounters*. New-York ; London : Routledge. Online.

Leeds-Hurwitz, Wendy. 1988. "La Quête Des Structures :
Gregory Bateson Et l'Histoire Naturelle d'un Entre-
tien." In *Bateson : Premier État d'un Héritage*, edited by
Yves Winkin, 67–77. Paris : Éditions du Seuil.

McQuown, Norman A, ed. 1971. *The Natural History of an
Interview*. Vol. 95–98. Microfilm Collection of Manuscripts on Cultural Anthropology. Chicago : University
of Chicago Library. Online.

Merzeau, Louise. 2009. "Du Signe à La Trace : L'information Sur Mesure." *Hermes, La Revue* n° 53 (1) : 21–29.
Online.

Paveau, Marie-Anne. 2017. *L'analyse Du Discours Numérique : Dictionnaire Des Formes Et Des Pratiques*. Paris : Hermann. Online.

Vygotski, Lev. 1985. *Pensée Et Langage*. Paris : Messidor.

Theoretical and methodological framework for visual reflexive ethology

Christine Develotte
Morgane Domanchin
Samira Ibnelkaïd

The research presented in this book is based on an interdisciplinary approach to multimodal and multisemiotic interactional data. The polyartefacted seminar analysed here is the subject of a multidimensional study, which in our approach required audiovisual access to the sequences of verbal and non-verbal actions of the participants. This involves adopting a comprehensive ethological approach (Cosnier 1978), i.e., a "direct observation of behaviours experienced in the here and now" (Cosnier 2013, 258), taking into account interactional events as much as affects and empathic processes (Cosnier 2013).

In this chapter, we introduce the theoretical and methodological foundations underlying the collection, selection and analysis of this corpus of audiovisual data. We also justify our interest in this field of research leading to the emergence of what we call a "visual ethology".

Theoretical and methodological choices

Ethology as a global approach to the field

Jacques Cosnier [18], a researcher and one of the founders of a laboratory in Lyon [19], chose ethology to describe situations involving interpersonal communication (1978; 1986; 1987). Based on a descriptive analysis of human behaviour, this approach also includes individuals' points of view observed through interviews.

---

18. Jacques Cosnier was originally trained as a biologist.

19. Communication ethology laboratory, the foundation of the current ICAR laboratory.

Cosnier has called this naturalistic approach "comprehensive ethology".

Taking up this ethological perspective, we have sought here to develop a new approach : "visual reflexive ethology". Our new approach deals with video interaction data and is applied to ourselves, thereby integrating the advantages and limitations due to the fact that the ethologist and their object are intertwined and that, in this case, the interviews were conducted between and among ourselves.

Collecting data for each of the sessions naturally modified the traditional seminar environment by adding microphones and cameras which, by their presence, could influence the participants' behaviour. Our research takes this factor into account; it does not invalidate our naturalistic approach, which is accomplished precisely through the recording of our behaviour.

This approach requires making informed technical choices regarding the number of cameras and their location. We relied on the ICAR laboratory's expertise when dealing with such matters. The visual reflexive ethological appraoch takes its place in a landscape of human and social sciences delineated by visual ethnography and interactional analysis.

Visual ethnography

In our view, the complexity of studying the presence of subjects on a screen requires a multimodal and multisemiotic approach. Therefore, we draw on visual ethnography (Ruby 1996; Banks and Morphy 1997; Pink 2007; Dion 2007) to explore the general ecology of physical-digital interactions and to explore the flow of these interactions across different media platforms and formats. In order to do so, we make use of digital tools available to researchers in digital humanities (digital cameras, dynamic screen captures, video editing software, etc.). This approach allows us to study both verbal and non-verbal communicative behaviours on and off screen, and leads us to understand onscreen presence as a linguistic, sensory and technical phenomenon.

Within visual methods, video recording is more than a data collection tool – it is a technology involved in negotiating social relations [20] and a medium through which ethnographic knowledge is produced (Pink 2007, 173). Moreover, new digital technologies, interfaces and sociodigital networks are gradually introducing ethnographic studies of the everyday digital communication practices of individuals and communities (Pink 2007, 197). In addition to visual ethnography, a form of digital ethnography that is delinearised, multimodal and multisemiotic is emerging (Pink 2007, 197).

Interactional analysis

The notion of interaction has more or less restricted definitions depending on one's approach towards it. Goffman, a linguist and sociologist, and one of the founders of interaction analysis, explains that :

> Interaction (i.e., face-to-face interaction) is defined as the reciprocal influence of individuals upon one another's actions when in one another's immediate physical presence (Goffman 1973, 23).

The overall conversational resources thus inform us about the activity that the participants construct, from turn-taking to the overall structure of the interaction. They result in the definition of the content, form and the modalities of

---

20. Technology can only be used in the field if there is informed cooperation and explicit negotiations with the participants in order to establish a relationship of trust that is essential for the ethical constitution of the interactional dataset.

presence brought into play. Some of the chapters presented here will analyse the participants' language productions from an interactionist perspective initiated by Goffman, Sacks, Schegloff and Jefferson, and then pursued, by Cosnier, Kerbrat-Orecchioni, Véronique Traverso and Lorenza Mondada in France. In addition, the research gathered here aims at extending this interactionist approach by studying the impact of the screen on interactional rituals observed off-screen until now. This volume describes "the boundary between new practices and normative structures, as well as the appropriation by human actors of both the tools and the discursive or semiotic practices they induce" (Develotte, Kern, and Lamy 2011, 19).

A transdisciplinary approach : Visual reflexive ethology

We have chosen to employ a video-based approach to record, analyse and illustrate interactional phenomena [21]. Therefore, we chose not to transcribe verbal productions complemented with gesture-related annotations in the tradition of Conversation Analysis (initially based on audio recordings). Instead, we aimed at preserving the primary audiovisual material and guiding the reader-observer via a semiotic and narrative enrichment process applied in postproduction. The video thus constitutes a mode of analytical representation in itself which follows a scenario established beforehand by the researcher. Video clips as dynamic illustrations are thus an innovative way of displaying data analyses and contributing to the renewal of the study of social interactions by making use of the technological tools available to researchers in digital humanities.

Beyond this general theoretical-methodological framework, the authors of the different chapters of this book

---

21. Supplemented by semi-guided and explanatory interviews.

have chosen other frameworks specifically adapted to their topic and presented in each chapter. The fact that we call upon different fields in our analyses implies that the same concepts are sometimes used differently depending on the chosen approach.

Material situation

In this section, we will first describe the "digital ecosystem" (Bourassa 2018) of the seminar, emphasizing its material and human dimensions. The concept of digital ecosystem allows us to think of contexts as sites where multiple actors, both human and non-human, come into play, linked by organic, technical and dynamic relationships.

In the case of our seminar, the face-to-face and remote dimensions are intertwined through communication tools and artefacts.

Spatial organisation

The Pedagogical and Digital Innovation Room (LiPeN)

The "Screen-based Multimodal Interactions" (IMPEC[22]) seminar was held at the École Normale Supérieure (ENS) in Lyon in a room used for teaching workshops. The open-plan room contained mobile and modular furniture[23].

In the recorded sessions, depending on the session[24], the remote participants were located in London (UK), Hangzhou (China), Besançon, Caen and Aix-en-Provence (France). As they were geographically spread around the globe, they used various artefacts to communicate.

---

22. Interactions Multimodales Par ÉCrans (IMPEC).

23. The room is called LiPeN : "Laboratoire d'Innovation Pédagogique et Numérique" (Pedagogical and Digital Innovation Room)

24. See Introduction.

Remote communication artefacts and their positions in the room

In this book we differentiate between the notions of "set-up", "artefact" and "platform". By set-up, we mean the organisation of multiple artefacts and the use of different platforms to produce forms of presence.

The data collection set-up included microphones and video cameras to record interactional data.

Project timeline

The general research program was set as follows :

- — 2016–2017 — research design and data collection;
- — 2017-2018 — data processing, archiving, choice of research directions, initial brainstorming on the editorialisation process;
- — 2018-2019 — data analysis and book writing, further reflections on the online publication;
- — 2019-2020 — online editorialisation and opening access of the *Ortolang* database containing this research corpus to the scientific public.

Two data sets

Two types of data were collected and will be presented in the following sections : first, the interactional data, and then the data from interviews conducted with the participants.

Interactional data

During the 2016-2017 academic year, the choice of five seminar sessions was based on varying the communication situations as much as possible. We sought to place the guest lecturers alternately in face-to-face and remote situations (remotely via Beam or the Kubi robot or, in person, in Lyon), so as to multiply the communication scenarios to be studied [25]. We also tried to vary different criteria, such as the status of each speaker (doctoral student or senior researcher).

Data on participants' affects

The interviews were mainly audio or video recorded. According to the research perspective being adopted, two types of methodologically different interviews were conducted : explicitation interviews (Vermersch 1994) and semiguided interviews to clarify specific aspects.

Other data collections related to individual perceptions were conducted in writing at the end of each session in order to evaluate participants' feelings of co-presence. This type of data was collected asynchronously and hence mirrors a deeper reflective approach. In total, 4 questions were related to the participants' feelings.

In addition, 18 audio and video interviews were transcribed and reviewed by the participant in question [26].

Data collection set-up

Five of the ten sessions from 2016–2017 were selected to constitute the research corpus which has a total duration of 9 hours and 16 minutes. Each session was filmed in Lyon from three to four different angles, and two to four different sound recordings were produced. In addition, at least two video recordings were collected at each session to document the behaviour of the remote participants through dynamic screen captures or external videos. These data can be arranged in a multi-screen format and, depending on the analysis, certain aspects can be zoomed in.

---

25. See section on the "Specificities of a reflexive study".

26. For the participants, multiple experiences were often not possible. Only a few were able to experience the use of all the remote communication artefacts.

Data collection

The first step involved identifying sites and selecting the technical equipment to be used for the data collection (i.e., microphones, a webcam and video cameras). The purpose was to collect a large amount of footage that would be relevant for our research objectives.

The following choices were made :

— Between two and three fixed video cameras on tripods were placed around the room to provide both an overall view and a view centred on the video-projected slide show,

— A GoPro action video camera was used to capture an "overhead" view of the room. The same camera was sometimes placed in front of the Kubi robot when it was in use,

— A 360° video camera was placed in the centre of the room,

— Four microphones were placed around the horseshoe-shaped table.

Post-production work

After each data collection, each recording source (audio, video, screen capture, remote view) was processed and synchronised with the same time scale (also called a "time code").

This synchronisation helps to facilitate and enrich the analysis of phenomena by integrating different viewpoints (for instance, in-situ and ex-situ). Subsequently, the audio and video data were edited using Final Cut Pro X and Quick-Time Pro software. The video clips chosen were multiscope (combining several shooting angles on the same screen) in which six to eight views were selected and combined simultaneously. During the production of these videos, the audio sources were integrated into the video files [27] to provide better distribution of the sound. These initial edited video clips formed the basis for the research subgroups' analyses. In total, the "Digital Presences" corpus includes :

— 7 hours of video recordings (duration of the five sessions),
— 35 hours of video recordings, including all views,
— 10 hours of dynamic screen captures,
— 28 hours of audio recordings

Data storage

The data has been stored in the *Ortolang* database which will be presented in "Document sharing tools". In order to make it easier to share data among group members, the digitised sound and video data were classified and listed according to a nomenclature that made them easy to find. The data were then stored in folders associated with each of the five sessions presented above (i.e., IMPEC_LiPeN-year-month-day). A summary data sheet containing a brief description of all the views available is included in each of the data collections.

Developing synopses and setting up a collective workspace

During our meetings, we sought to establish an effective methodology to collectively annotate our data. We thus created "synopsis" files in digital workspaces (Google Drive) which were accessible to the whole group, in which each person was asked to enter events that were particularly relevant to their research focus.

---

27. For example, unlike.mp4 files, .mov files using QuickTime Pro software allow researchers to check or uncheck an audio track. In the event of overlap between participants, for example, this feature allows one of the unchecked audio tracks to be silenced and can be useful for transcribing speaking turns.

Transcripts

We transcribed the discussions that followed the talks in order to see how each of the artefacts we used took part in the exchanges, and the effects their presence had on the interactions. We opted for a minimal transcription limited to the verbal cues, providing a first "basic" transcript. The 18 (audio and video) interviews conducted with each participant from the research group were transcribed in the same way. These transcripts allowed the group to study the 14 hours and 36 minutes of audio recordings. The transcribed version of these interviews resulted in a 231-page transcript booklet, in which the transcripts were arranged in chronological order. This booklet was produced and distributed to the various participants in May 2019 and later on was released to the public.

The decision-making process and organisation of discussions

Participants' roles in the seminar

Apart from the role of the seminar leader mentioned by Christine in the Introduction, other roles were assigned while still others emerged spontaneously during the sessions. The organisation of the seminar – both logistically and technically – was ensured by its members.

For example, Morgane, a doctoral student in Lyon who is highly involved in the life of the ICAR laboratory, supported the technical set-up of the room hand-in-hand with the members of the *Cellule Corpus Complexes*. She also monitored the digitisation of the videos and transcribed the interviews. In addition to this "official" technical and methodological assistance, other types of support helped the operation to function properly [28].

Collaborative data collection and analysis

The choice was made to involve all participants in each and every stage of the research project. The contribution of its members resulted in the co-construction of the project, implying a collaborative consulting policy among members throughout the tasks and sub-tasks we encountered. The discussions related to decision-making took the form of brainstorming workshops, data sessions or even opinions written in emails in between sessions. The topics of the discussions included for instance the choice of the camera's location in the room in Lyon or the anonymisation or not of the data for the publications.

Document-sharing tools

A scientific repository platform

The Ortolang platform is a facility designed for language data storage and processing, supported by the Huma-Num infrastructure. Its aim is to construct a network infrastructure including a repository of language data (corpora, lexicons, dictionaries etc.) and readily available, well-documented tools for its processing.

This platform has hosted our data since the beginning of our project. It was chosen not only for its simplicity of use, user-friendly interface, and large storage capacity, but also for a feature which makes it possible to provide access to the corpus to various audiences, including researchers and

---

28. Dorothée was in charge of the Beam robot; Christelle set up the video-conferencing sessions on Adobe Connect and provided a space on *Ortolang* for our data storage; Caroline booked the material and the room, took notes on Google Doc and managed the Google Drive storage system.

even the general public [29]. This *open data* approach reflects this project's position supporting open science.

A shared space for non-sensitive data

We occasionally used Google Drive to store elements related to the project, especially to collaborate on publications, plan abstracts for conferences, comments on video extracts, etc. Google Documents was used for collective note-taking during the seminars, which were also archived on Google Drive. We also created and stored collaborative synopses associated with each session.

Writing process

The idea was to give an account of the group's experience in a diffracted way by highlighting different aspects that seemed the most interesting to prioritise in our project.

Group process

During the seminar, each of the sub-groups was asked to present their intended approach to the analyses, their theoretical-methodological angle and a few examples of relevant data. Each presentation led to numerous exchanges with the whole group, allowing certain points to be clarified and others to be enriched.

The feedback provided by the group throughout the writing process led to a two-day research workshop in June 2019 which focused on the first drafts of the various chapters.

---

29. Access the "Digital Presences" corpus on the *Ortolang* platform.

Specificities of a reflexive study

Using oneself as the object of study on a topic such as digital presences is by no means trivial. On the contrary, it generates effects that must be integrated into the analyses.

Reflexivity on the research purpose

The effects of familiarity with the subject suggest that the research results relate to a "non-naive" audience who may adopt more appropriate behaviours (e.g., in positioning themselves in relation to the webcam or using the chat function on Adobe Connect) than an unsuspecting audience. Moreover, neutrality becomes relative when the interviewers are close colleagues involved in the same project. It can be assumed that the preservation of each other's face is reinforced, especially when all parties know that everything said will be made public. The quality of the socio-affective relationship between the members of the group is taken into account in handling the data (especially regarding opinions collected in interviews and questionnaires).

Towards "visual ethology"

Through the theoretical and methodological framework presented in this chapter, we aim to lay the foundations of what we call "visual reflexive ethology". This research approach takes on a video-based methodology and places emphasis on the participants' (inter)subjective experience.

References

Banks, Marcus, and Howard Morphy, eds. 1997. *Rethinking Visual Anthropology*. New Haven : Yale University Press.

Bourassa, Renée. 2018. "Design Des Écosystèmes Numériques : Des Modèles Éditoriaux Stabilisés Vers l'intégration de La Conversation Scientifique." Lyon. Online.

Cosnier, Jacques. 1978. "Spécificité de l'attitude Étholo-
gique Dans l'étude Du Comportement Humain." *Psychologie Française* 23 (1) : 19–26.

———. 1986. "Ethology : A Transdisciplinary Discipline."
In *Ethology and Psychology*, 19–28. Toulouse : Privat,
I.E.C. Online.

———. 1987. "L'éthologie Du Dialogue." In *Décrire La
Conversation*, edited by Jacques Cosnier and Catherine
Kerbrat-Orecchioni, 291–315. Linguistique Et Sémiolo-
gie : Travaux Du Centre de Recherches Linguistiques
Et Sémiologiques de l'Université de Lyon II. Lyon :
Presses universitaires de Lyon. Online.

———. 2013. "Cinquante Ans d'interactionnisme : Introduction Pour Une Éthologie Compréhensive. Écrits
Colligés (1963-2013)." Online.

Develotte, Christine, Richard Kern, and Marie-Noëlle
Lamy, eds. 2011. *Décrire La Conversation En Ligne : La
Face à Face Distanciel*. Lyon : ENS Éditions.

Dion, Delphine. 2007. "Les Apports de l'anthropologie Visuelle à l'étude Des Comportements de Consommation." *Recherche Et Applications En Marketing (French Edition)* 22 (1) : 61–78. Online.

Goffman, Erving. 1973. *La Présentation de Soi*. La Mise En
Scène de La Vie Quotidienne 1. Paris : Les Éditions de
Minuit. Online.

Pink, Sarah. 2007. *Doing Visual Ethnography : Images, Media,
and Representation in Research*. 2nd ed. London ; Thousand Oaks, Calif : Sage Publications.

Ruby, Jay. 1996. "Visual Anthropology." In *Encyclopedia of
Cultural Anthropology*, edited by David Levinson and
Melvin Ember, 4 :1345–51. New York : H. Holt.

Vermersch, Pierre. 1994. *L'entretien d'explicitation En Formation Initiale Et En Formation Continue*. Paris : ESF Éditeur.

Attentional affordances in an instrumented seminar

Mabrouka El Hachani
Jean-François Grassin
Joséphine Rémon
Caroline Vincent

Through a corpus study, we approach the seminar as a dual attentional system in its material construction of space and in its relational construction. In this context, we seek to describe the process of the co-construction of attention.

Our research question involves qualifying attention in a hybrid polyartefacted doctoral seminar. How is attention co-constructed and how do we recognise attentional phenomena in a context where their manifestations are dependent on artefaction?

Below, we discuss the concepts that have informed our approach to attention from an ecological perspective : attentional framing, the different modes of joint attention, attentional gestures and signs, the technogenesis of attention and attentional affordances.

Theoretical framework

The aim of this chapter is to observe and understand the "digital impregnation" of our attention, i.e., how the polyartefacted context recharacterises attention in a specific situation of joint and collaborative attention [30]. The situation involves the presence of people in a remote location which makes attentional regimes more complex. Our ecological perspective on attention will be a microeconomy [31] of joint attention (Citton 2014) including collective, artefacted and transindividual attentional regimes.

---

30. For an exploration of the collaborative processes at work, check "Research training in a polyartefacted doctoral seminar".

31. That is, considered at the level of situated activity.

The theoretical framework of our analysis is at the cross-roads of phenomenological analysis (Depraz 2014; Livet 2016) and theories of artefacted interactions (Arminen, Licoppe, and Spagnolli 2016). The situation we are interested in, that of a research seminar, touches on the analysis of professional situations (workplace studies) and training situations. Our approach is based on a phenomenological analysis, particularly of attention and affordances emerging in the situation, rather than on an analysis of the activity in all its dimensions.

The situation we are studying is a work meeting in which artefacts play an important organisational role. Our analysis is situated, but we believe it can be used to gain a more comprehensive understanding of a world in which we are increasingly caught up in "tightly interwoven networks of intertwined attentions[32]" (Citton 2014, 127) and in which artefacts are increasingly used in interactions. This use implies a growing variability in attentional capacities, attention being, moreover, "an intimate dimension of our humanity" (Depraz 2014).

In this sense, the perspective we adopt is resolutely ecological, supplementing a conception of attention focused on objects with a detailed attention to environments. To put it differently, the object takes on meaning for actors within a specific environment, and this meaning allows them to pay attention to it. The phenomenological viewpoint makes attention "an experience of openness to the world rather than an internal mental state" (Depraz 2014).

The artefactual situation we are dealing with does not ontologically change attention, but the multiplicity of possible targets for this attention complicates the "affective and attentional tunings" (Citton 2014) that are required for the joint activity expected in a research seminar : listening

---

32. We have translated all quotes by French speaking authors.

to speakers (Sessions 2 and 4), presenting research to the group (Sessions 1 and 5), and engaging in scientific discussions together (all sessions) are all activities whose scripts are relatively well known and expected by the participants.

Attentional framing

Our attentional framing is therefore a collaborative situation that involves joint attention. Natalie Depraz (2014) defines joint attention as "a structural case of relation to others via an object that is the tangible fuel of the relationship between two subjects, which builds intersubjectivity" (Depraz 2014, 410).

Co-attention or joint attention requires constant attentional feedback : to receive attention, one must pay attention.

The different modes of joint attention

Depraz identifies three modes of experiencing the articulation between attention and intersubjectivity, or three forms of co-attentionality that we explore here and illustrate with examples : intersubjective attention, attentional intersubjectivity and interattention.

Joint attention as an experience is not homogeneous : it can be emotional, rational, or complex. It is a "mode of presence to" another person, a situation, an event, etc. Attentional practices depend on different confrontations with other elements involved, each creating fragility : the environment, the situation, the activity, the people, the artefacts and the documents.

Within the seminar, the modes of co-attention took place within a specific organisational space which we analyse below.

The seminar as a space for attentional organisation : attentional gestures and signs

We understand the seminar as a form of organisational framing of attention in which :

> individually and collectively, individuals engage in a dynamic process of orienting attention, constructing meaning and developing appropriate responses (Rouby and Thomas 2014, 43).

Within this system of distributed attentional processing (Ocasio 2011, 1290), different types of behaviour (signal selection, interpretation, action) can occur.

Analysing the attentional frameworks we are interested in requires heuristic tools. Attention is indeed not a unitary concept but a variety of interrelated processes that we describe here. William Ocasio (2011) differentiates three forms of processes : attentional perspective, attentional engagement, and attentional selection.

Attentional perspective, individual or collective

Attentional perspective is shaped by experience and by the attentional roles assigned in the situation.

Attentional perspective determines, among other things, whether or not the attentional markers posed by the participants are taken into account. Thus, if the participants chose to orient their attentional perspective towards technical management, then alerts of this type would be noticed and dealt with as a priority.

Attentional engagement

Attentional engagement is an intentional and sustained process of allocating attention to solve a problem and make sense of a situation.

In the case of the seminar, attentional engagement manifested itself through the constantly renewed proxy of presence of one another through the available digital devices (guiding the Beam device, rotating the Kubi, activating a microphone, projecting onto the wall etc.). Attentional engagement took multiple forms, in a type of attentional flexibility, as defined by Évelyne Rouby and Catherine Thomas (2014).

Selective attention

The term selective attention refers to the process by which individuals direct information processing to a specific set of sensory stimuli at a given time.

The three processes described by Ocasio (2011) are among the heuristic tools that allow us to understand the attentional orchestration within the seminar and the technogenesis of attention. We explore below how the notion of affordances also contributes to this understanding.

Technogenesis of attention and attentional affordances

In the situation under study, artefacts are in the foreground and their role is crucial in terms of attentional frames.

Co-affordances

In our case, we cannot interpret individually the affordances of the connected objects that enable communication because we are engaged in collaborative work. The situation shapes scripts where action is collective and cognition is distributed. These scripts are largely emergent.

Furthermore, following Bruno Latour and Nicolas Guilhot (2007), we believe that "objects have the strange capacity to be both compatible with social competences at certain decisive moments, and the next moment, totally alien to the repertoire of human action" (Latour and Guilhot 2007, 284), and that the situation therefore involves a high level of uncertainty.

This has two main consequences :

— We need to consider affordances in relation to groups and communities of individuals, so as to better take into account the co-influence between individuals, groups and their social and material environment; we call these social affordances "co-affordances".

— Communicative objects serve co-presence, and their affordances are above all attentional. The set-up we are studying is thus composed of human and non-human elements, and in this sense, it is heterogeneous because all of the technical artefacts aim to support communication and interaction between individuals within the framework of the research seminar. We call the set-up in question "attentional" (attentional set-up) because it appears to support the attention required for exchange and interaction.

These two characteristics of the affordances of telepresence artefacts and software are our focus in this chapter, specifically, their co-construction and their relationship with attention.

Corpus analysis : co-construction of the attentional set-up

Here we describe the complexity of the seminar process through the analysis of the sessions and interviews with the participants.

A complex system

The complexity of the set-up is based on several aspects that we will analyse and explain below : the multiplicity of attentional foci, the complexity of the participation framework, a deficit of perceptibility and the fact that the perspectives of each person are difficult to interchange. We will see that the bidirectional circulation of attention (reciprocal attention to others), attentional intersubjectivity, is the most challenging characteristic of joint attention in the polyartefacted set-up. The non-reciprocity of perspectives makes interactions more complex.

Multiple foci of attention

The complexity of attentional orchestration within the seminar is due, first of all, to the multiplicity of attentional foci. The participants needed to pay attention to the conditions that made the interaction possible (the technical set-up), but also to the main object of the seminar, a talk for example, and to the interactional felicity (Cosnier 2008) of each participant in the group.

The multiplicity of focus points is combined with an audiovisual complexity which means that the participants do not have a comprehensive understanding of how the system works at any given time.

Audio-visual complexity

In Session 2, we can see an example of how complex the set-up is. The origin of the sound is difficult to identify, even for the participants themselves, who do not know which artefact is sending the sound to the remote participants, making attention allocation and interactional ratification more difficult.

At any given moment, the participants do not necessarily have a clear idea of how the set-up works, i.e., which artefacts are sending sound and image to the remote participants. This complicates the attentional choreographies (Jones 2004, 28) and requires the reconstruction of a collective and distributed apprehension of affordances, i.e., mutually recognised possibilities of action for each participant, which we call attentional co-affordances.

The examples taken from the corpus show the complexity of a situation where collaborative orchestration is made necessary by the absence of a comprehensive understanding of the system by each individual.

False affordances

Hidden affordances (Gaver 1991) outline a non-participation framework or a framework of non-ratification, due to technical problems or unperceived possibilities of action. This impediment, which stems from the constitutive assymmetry of the situation, requires co-construction in order to circumvent obstacles.

In our case, false affordances are those imagined about the perspective of others. For example, I may think that the Beam robot can easily be moved to follow face-to-face speech, when in fact it cannot. Or I may think that when I speak to participants using Adobe Connect, I should look at the wall where their image is projected. But this projected presence is a false affordance as you would actually have to look at the camera that is filming the room in Lyon to appear to be speaking directly to participants.

Lack of mutual recognition

To add to the complexity of the situation, in the presence of kinetic-audio-visual impediments, participants do not know whether they are dealing with a deliberate choice on the part of the remote participant (for example, she has momentarily turned off her microphone to speak with someone at home), non-ratification (are the participants on Adobe silent because they have not been given the floor, because they cannot hear what is being said in person, or because they have been forgotten by the participants in Lyon?) or a technical problem (for example, are the remote participants silent because there is a momentary problem with the sound in the webcast, or because they have no contribution to make at that moment?).

We can see that the lack of reciprocity in the perception of the situation leads the participants to wonder how they should manage interactions with each other[33].

Non-reciprocity of perspectives

The main feature that is challenged in the definition of co-attention that we gave earlier is the reciprocity of perceptions.

Joint attention requires the mutually explicit perceptibility of the affordances at stake in the polyartefacted situation we are analysing, i.e., each participant must be aware of the possibilities offered to the other by the environment and vice versa. This awareness is not simple because the situation is new to the participants who are not used to all the artefacts. The co-constructed intelligibility of affordances is at the heart of the hybrid seminar as well as of our study because it makes joint attention possible. In a situation where it is difficult to put oneself in another's shoes, especially when one has never used an artefact before (how can one know that on the Kubi, the angle of vision is reduced or needs to be adjusted if the artefact is moved manually?), each participant's possibilities of action must be made explicit.

The non-reciprocity of perspectives constitutive of the system

The "Digital Presences" experimental set-up was constitutively dissymmetrical from the point of view of each person's perspective. This is precisely why the attentional set-up needed to be constructed or reconstructed. This assymmetry of

---

33. Check "New norms of politeness in digital contexts")

perspectives can be explained from the point of view of empathy.

In our set-up, there was a constitutive assymmetry due to the fact that not all the artefacts had been tested by all the participants. The non-interchangeability of points of view was as much physical as mental, as it was difficult to know what was relevant from an attentional point of view for the Beam pilot without having used the artefact oneself.

For example, during Session 5, Christelle (the Kubi pilot) asks the participants in Lyon to reposition the camera sending the video to the remote participants because she cannot see what is happening in the room. The participants in Lyon do this only because Christelle has asked them to.

In the interview conducted with Amélie by Dorothée and Samira, this assymmetry also appears in terms of sound. Amélie recalls a moment when she sneezed, and she did not realise that the sound effect in Lyon was dramatically amplified because of the adjustment of the microphones at that moment. This detail may seem like a non-event, but it had an impact on the group's thought process and understanding of each other's attentional perspectives.

Affordance blindness

From the point of view of the attentional orchestration, this affordance blindness complicates the co-construction of the set-up. By affordance blindness, we mean the absence of awareness of a possibility of action : Amélie is not aware that the volume of the sound transmitted is high even though technically this possibility of action is available. Amélie participates in this construction later on by turning off her microphone, when necessary, as she explains in an interview : "Afterwards, this was useful for the following seminars, I turned off my microphone so that when I sneezed no one could hear me".

This time, a strong signal was not given to her by the participants during the interaction, but by the research data, in this case the research videos she had started to watch.

View could also be affected by affordance blindness. Amélie comments on the situation when the speakers moved the table closer to the microphones (Session 2). She found herself wedged between their table and the participants' table in Lyon behind her.

She herself cannot rely on her perception of distance; she is both the most geographically distant participant and the closest from a proxemic point of view, a proximity that is uncomfortable for her. She is aware, at the time of the interview, which takes place one month after this session, of the non-reciprocity of these aspects.

Attentional orchestration

In view of the complexity described above, we can hypothesise that attentional orchestration is constructed by placing successive attentional markers during the interaction. This allows participants to orient the attentional selection process of the entire group, or a few members.

Placement of attentional markers

We define this marking as the production of a weak or strong attentional signal through discourse or gestures. The marker indicates "mutually explicit" affordance attention (to use Depraz's terminology) at a given moment. This marker may or may not be taken up again spontaneously, depending on one's role and contextual and temporal priorities. We see in the two examples below that a marker can be produced but not taken up immediately when the imperatives and constituents of the interaction conflict with the co-affordance to be constructed (for example, taking into account the poor sound quality for remote participants).

In Session 2, a cue is given regarding the fact that Tatiana cannot hear, following a signal taken up by Josephine from the Adobe chat projected on the wall.

This cue is not picked up on by Christine, after the initial adjustments are made, as her priority is to ensure that the guest speakers can give their talk, which is also being filmed in order to be posted on the IMPEC website. Moreover, the investment in human and material resources in setting up the system makes any malfunctioning problematic, as it is not a set-up that is easy to reproduce outside of a planned event established well in advance.

Conversely, during Session 5, once the attention is focused on the problem of Christelle's view of the room, Jean-François then spontaneously checks that she can correctly see what is happening in Lyon without her reminding him. In this session, there is no external guest participating in the seminar, which also gives the participants more room to rework attentional markers.

A certain fluidity can even be observed, i.e., the interaction does not stop during a readjustment of the possibilities of action. For example, during this same session, Jean-François gets up to adjust the position of the camera filming the Kubi in the room in Lyon. He does so while contributing to the interaction about the diagram being drawn on the board by Caroline.

Thus, negative affordances (Gibson 1979) for some represent the possibility for others of placing attentional markers which ultimately contribute to the co-construction of the overall attentional set-up.

An example of the attentional affordances of the set-up : projection of the screen presence of the Adobe interface

Putting people on the screen affords their presence. Projecting their image on a wall was an active element of the seminar. Their projections allowed the participants to be present to the others and was a very strong attentional focus, perceptible through gestures (pointing gestures) and verbalisations interpreting what was projected (notably when the participants' image was frozen). This set-up provided attentional affordances, but also false affordances.

Through its salience, the projection of the Adobe screen both directed attention and projected the presence of the connected participants. But the projections also introduced false affordances, directing the gaze and speech towards images and not people.

During Susan Herring's lecture (Session 6), Christelle was connected to Adobe and her image was projected on the wall. As Susan Herring, piloting a Beam robot, answered a question asked by Christelle, she wanted to direct her "body" towards her and, to do so, she directed the robot towards the projected image of Christelle on the wall.

This example illustrates various phenomena that we have demonstrated in this chapter : the lack of symmetry of perceptions, the collective construction of the affordance network providing the fluidity of interactions, false accessibilities to others, the need to make one's intentions and perceptions explicit to others, and finally, the assumption of responsibility for interattention by the group. We see in the following section that the assumption of responsibility for interattention involves the construction of attentional co-affordances.

Emergence of attentional co-affordances

A trace of the construction of attentional co-affordances appears in Session 5. Christelle points out that Tatiana has posted in the chat, Morgane reads aloud what Tatiana has written, and Jean-François replies aloud to Tatiana without her having spoken. He is, however, explicitly addressing her. This exchange illustrates an example of a redefinition of mutually-explicit attention, which no longer involves *gaze awareness*, the awareness of the direction of the gaze, but *attention awareness*, the awareness of the focus of attention. Jean-François' co-affordance action is validated since Tatiana confirms that she has heard his proposal and the exchange that followed. Thus, the trust that Jean-François showed towards the affordance co-construction appears to be legitimate.

In this session, the last one filmed for the research corpus, mutually explicit attention is no longer based on the convergence of gazes, but on affordance co-construction. The participants make a constantly renewed and gradually less risky bet that the attentional orchestration can be built on a non-reciprocity of perspectives, affordances and gazes.

The "Digital Presences" set-up brings into play our own and others' perceptibility. Our analysis has brought to light the collective and co-constructed understanding of potentialities in a polyartefacted situation as well as the fact that this understanding requires an attentional orchestration which is itself co-elaborated. This reciprocal accommodation in an artefacted environment leads to a distinction between awareness of the direction of each other's gaze or gestures, and awareness of each other's attentional focus. The hybrid artefacted environment thus leads to the exploration of other ways of enabling the projection and awareness of attention. For instance, we learned to interact in the seminar without mutually-explicit attention as defined by Depraz, all the while remaining confident in the interaction. We can hypothesise that trust in the co-affordance construct takes the place of mutually-explicit attention. This is a kind of meta-vigilance as described by Livet (2016) : a vigilance to our lack of vigilance or to our attentional neglect. In our view, the effort involved in such an attentional set-up requires individuals to build a collective capable of managing the variety of our attentional neglects, and to be more sensitive to them, in order to manage collective action and participation.

This effort is a dynamic process that leads to the emergence of attentional co-affordances.

Attentional co-affordances enable co-presence and attentional orchestration. The perceptibility of these affordances is apprehended collaboratively through the placement of attentional markers, until mutually-explicit attention is achieved despite the assymmetry of perspectives within the media space.

References

Arminen, Ilkka, Christian Licoppe, and Anna Spagnolli. 2016. "Respecifying Mediated Interaction." *Research on Language and Social Interaction* 49 (4) : 290–309. Online.

Citton, Yves. 2014. *Pour Une Écologie de l'attention.* Paris : Éditions du Seuil. Online.

Cosnier, Jacques. 2008. "Les Gestes Du Dialogue." In *La Communication, État Des Savoirs*, edited by Philippe Cabin and Jean-François Dortier, 119–28. Auxerre : Éditions Sciences Humaines. Online.

Depraz, Natalie. 2014. *Attention Et Vigilance : À La Croisée de La Phénoménologie Et Des Sciences Cognitives.* Épiméthée. Paris : Presses universitaires de France. Online.

Gaver, William W. 1991. "Technology Affordances." In *Proceedings of the SIGCHI Conference on Human Factors in Computing Systems Reaching Through Technology - CHI '91*, 79–84. New Orleans, Louisiana : ACM Press. Online.

Gibson, James J. 1979. *The Ecological Approach to Visual Perception.* Boston : Houghton Mifflin.

Jones, Rodney. 2004. "The Problem of Context in Computer-Mediated Communication Communication." In *Dis-*

course and Technology : Multimodal Discourse Analysis, edited by Philip LeVine and Ron Scollon, 20–33. Washington, D.C : Georgetown University Press. Online.

Latour, Bruno, and Nicolas Guilhot. 2007. *Changer de Société, Refaire de La Sociologie*. Paris : Éditions La Découverte. Online.

Livet, Pierre. 2016. "Vigilances Et Négligences." *Intellectica. Revue de l'Association Pour La Recherche Cognitive* 66 (2) : 81–99. Online.

Ocasio, William. 2011. "Attention to Attention." *Organization Science* 22 (5) : 1286–96. Online.

Rouby, Évelyne, and Catherine Thomas. 2014. "La Construction de Compétences Collectives En Environnement Complexe : Une Analyse En Termes d'attention Organisationnelle. Le Cas Exploratoire de La Conduite d'un Four de Cimenterie." *@GRH* 12 (3) : 39–74. Online.

Artefacted intercorporeality, between reification and personification

Samira Ibnelkaïd
Dorothée Furnon

> And to say that things are structures, frameworks,
> the stars of our life : not before us, laid out as
> perspective spectacles, but gravitating around us
> (Merleau-Ponty 1960, 269).

The new technobodily modalities of onscreen presence invite us to reconceptualise the foundations of the Goffmanian definition of interaction as "the reciprocal influence of individuals upon one another's actions when in one another's immediate physical presence" (Goffman 1973). It follows from this definition that notions of presence, intersubjectivity ("reciprocal influence"), corporeality ("physical") and agency ("respective actions") ought to be revisited in light of new sociodigital practices.

During their onscreen interactions – here, notably, using a telepresence robot – individuals undertake actions whose authors are difficult to identify. Agency (Butler 2002) is distributed between subject and *tekhnê* and produces a potential indeterminacy in the assignability of the ethical responsibility of action. Between the locutor, the artefact and the interlocutor, the question arises as to the attribution of the interactional gesture : from its intention to its emission and its perception. All the more so since, although the interaction may be symmetrical in nature (Maingueneau 1996), interactivity (Weissberg 2002) appears to be unilateral. Thus, the pilot of the robot can undertake a series of actions and create a meaningful context that the interlocutor cannot technically regulate (interactivity of the software in transmission and non-interactivity of the hardware in reception [34]). This asymmetry of the interactivity with the artefact introduces an illusionary confusion between subject and object, which are mistaken for one another, assimilated to one and another, or substituted for one another. As a consequence, the intersubjective, technical, and corporeal modalities of presence are affected.

The definition of the body – the interface of interactions – is thus at stake. The body, in fact, acts as a mediator. During online interactions, one's body is sometimes visible, often partially perceptible and in all cases elusive. It should therefore be noted that :

> What happens with the advent of digitalisation is a complex hybridisation between thought and gesture, between the computer-object and the user-subject who deploys a skilful and unsystematic know-how, which falls under vagueness, under approximation, under creative improvisation as much as under routines (Frias 2004, 10).

It is thus essential to explore the new practical technobodily modalities enacted in a hybrid and polyartefacted presence. Our aim is to analyse, from an interactionist and phenomenological perspective, the epistemological and ethical stakes involved in a form of extended presence that entails both the reification of living subjects and the personification of communicational artefacts. This is a process that is involved in the co-construction of an intercorporeality, of an interworld.

---

34. On the Beam, the user can, for example, raise or lower the volume of their microphone on the interface, whereas the interlocutor, facing the robot, cannot control the output volume (unlike on Skype, for example, which allows the volume to be controlled "from both sides").

The technobodily modalities of (onscreen) interaction

Interaction and subjects of action

During their interaction with others, individuals produce multimodal actions for which they are held responsible. This capacity of a subject to act on their environment, on objects and on others, as well as the subject's perception of this faculty, is subsumed under the notion of agency (Butler 2002).

Agency (our acts, our thoughts, our desires are ours and we are relatively conscious of causing and controlling them) combined with resonance (the automatic, non-conscious capacity that pushes us to make the emotions of others resonate in ourselves) and empathy (the active process of understanding the cause of the emotional state of others and displaying understanding and acknowledgement of their emotions) constitute the three dimensions of interaction that allow interactants to build social ties and ensure group cohesion, as well as the autonomy of each individual with respect to others (Nadel and Decety 2006). Individuals are indeed connected to one another by resonance and empathy : resonance makes them automatically reflect the attitudes and expressions of others, and empathy allows them to partially feel what others are experiencing (Tisseron et al. 2013), so that they can, for example, provide help. On the other hand, agency ensures that every individual is the master of their actions, thus avoiding all confusion between self and other.

Yet this distinction is more difficult to make when a form of mediation between the production of an action and its perception by others comes into play. During an onscreen interaction, for instance, the locutor physically produces multimodal activities that a digital artefact partially retransmits to the interlocutor. The elements appearing on the interlocutor's screen can be defined as "indexes" of action as described by Charles Sanders Peirce (1960). The restitution of the elements of action is jointly accomplished by the digital tool and the user and is subject to media affordances. These affordances "come into play during an instrumented activity and are defined as the set of possibilities and constraints of the environment that give agents different options to act" (Lamy 2010, 3).

Individuals and their communicational artefacts have recourse to both natural and non-natural language as a tool of mediation and intercession by mobilising all the semiotic resources at their disposal to act on one another (De Fornel 2013). The notion of agency in the field of anthropology also sheds valuable light on the distinction in the attribution of responsibility for an action between subject and object. Anthropology brings about a decentring of the intentional human subject in favour of a multiplicity of agents, whether human or non-human (De Fornel 2013).

The corporeality of (inter)action

Whatever the nature of agency, carrying out an action necessarily involves a prior corporeal activity, whether the latter is synchronous or asynchronous, self-initiated or other-initiated. Social interactions are by nature body-to-body interactions (Cosnier 2004), since in fact "if the locutor thinks and speaks with their body, the interlocutor also perceives and interprets with their body" (Cosnier 2004). Here we propose to rethink corporeality in social interactions from a phenomenological approach insofar as the etymological origin of the term "phenomenon" is found in the Greek verb φαινεσθαι : to appear, to be shown. Appearing prefigures the moment when the subject and the object or the others come into contact : their decisive "taking cognizance" (Heidegger 1985). As Maurice Merleau-Ponty explains in his *Phenomenology of Perception* (1945), the body cannot be regarded as an object of the world, but rather as the means for our communication with it.

Despite these considerations, phenomenological studies have focused their attention so far on the relationship between the Self and the Other and between the Self and the object, neglecting the technical mediation of interindividual relationships. However, as Stéphane Vial notes, "in itself, every phenomenon is phenomenotechnological. There is a transcendental technicality of appearing : i.e., an a priori technical dimension in every phenomenal manifestation or 'phany' " (2013, 152). For an Other or an object to appear to a Self and vice versa, a technical mediation is indeed required, whatever its form. Gaston Bachelard's phenomenotechnique reminds us that an "ontophany" – the manifestation of a being – requires a technology as much to occur as to be observed.

With the advent of new technologies, some perceive the body as "an unworthy archaeological vestige that is destined to disappear" (Le Breton 2001, 20). The relationship between the body and technologies attracts fascination and concern insofar as it evokes the myth of a spirit that is separated from the body, of an artificial being that the savant would be able to create, of perfect communication without misunderstanding (Flichy 2009, 11). This crisis of sensibility of the body involves a tension between two different ways of relating to the body : namely, the tension between a biomechanical view inherited from modernity and a virtual view of the body that comes from postmodernity (Casilli 2012, 6). However, the fear of the body disappearing, "swallowed up by a computer screen is less a real risk than a paradoxical reaction to its imaginary hypertrophy, its omnipresence" and this is because our society elevates the body to the status of the ultimate referent (Casilli 2009, 3). Inasmuch as digital ontophany has a broad impact on the phe-nomenological presence of the things themselves, this is not a matter of the body disappearing but of new forms of corporeal appearance (Vial 2013, 239).

Analysis of sequences of personification and reification

Scientific positioning

Our analytical approach to technobodily modalities of enacting onscreen intersubjectivity is based on an inter-disciplinary methodology drawing on visual ethnography (Banks and Morphy 1997; Ruby 2000; Pink 2007; Dion 2007, etc.), multimodal interaction analysis (Goffman 1973; Cosnier 2004; Mondada 2008; Kerbrat-Orecchioni 2010; Traverso 2012, etc.) and phenomenology (Husserl 1929; Merleau-Ponty 1945; Le Breton 2001; Vial 2013, etc.). The aim is to analyse sequences of social interac-tions from the participants' subjective experience : from their perception and their corporeal action both on and off screen. Our focus is on the participants' use of multi-modal resources related to corporeality (verbal resources, gesture, expressions, gaze, postures) and the multisemio-tic resources related to the media (pictures, graphics, vi-deos, links, techno-discursivity). Our audiovisual analysis of interactions is based on recordings that constitute both the medium and the object of an intrinsic analysis (embed-ded transcription and semiotic enrichment[35]). The aim is to study the participants' technobodily behaviour in poly-artefacted interactions both on and off screen.

---

35. Semiotic enrichment consists of denoting the participants' technobodily activities by embedding signs in the audio-visual do-cument. It participates in the visual ethnographic approach which treats the image as an intrinsic element of the research process.

States of mediation

Here we focus on problematic interactional sequences occurring during the seminar sessions. These sequences were subject to faulty mediation or faulty apprehension of this mediation that lead to a suspension of the ordinary course of action.

We identify several stages in the mediation process in a problematic situation. Firstly, there is demediation when an incident occurs : communication is no longer ensured, and the medium no longer fulfils its role and fails to serve its purposes. Secondly, remediation attempts are made, wherein the incident is dealt with, mediation is repaired, and the medium can be relaunched, replaced, or supplemented. Finally, immediation occurs as soon as the incident has been resolved : the medium once again fulfils its purposes, and communication is transparent and creates the illusion of immediate communication.

Actions are thus undertaken by the interactants to provide technobodily mediation using multimodal and multisemiotic resources. Moreover, these actions are instantiated during the mediation process by the subjects, the latter embodying particular functions at specific moments in the interaction that we identify as follows. Sentinels ensure participants' extended presence and flag mediation incidents to the procurators. They are on the lookout for signs of demediation. The procurators are at the heart of the mediation process and ensure the presence of the interactants in a technobodily manner. They bring about remediation. Witnesses attend the interactional event and contribute to extended presence without directly intervening. They benefit from immediation.

The identification of these instances and states of mediation enables us to better understand the practical technobodily modalities of onscreen presence in the sequences that follow and, more specifically, the effects of personification and reification that they induce. Phenomena of the personification of artefacts refer to situations in which subjects attribute human properties to the concrete objects of mediation, endowing them with volition, power, the capacity to act, etc. Phenomena of reification of living beings, on the other hand, consist of regarding the other as an object, removing their human qualities and running the risk of negating all forms of empathy. These phenomena can be conscious or unconscious, intentional or unintentional.

A dual movement at work in artefactual intercorporeality

We have analysed three interactional sequences in which a personification of artefacts occurs (the analysis is available in the digital version of this manuscript) :
— Sequence 1 – Humorous attribution of a participant's sneezing to her robot
— Sequence 2 – Conferring agency to the robot during the distribution of speaking turns
— Sequence 3 – Simulation of an act of physical closing (a kiss on the cheek) addressed to artefacted participants

We then looked at three interactional sequences in which living beings are reified (the analysis is available in the digital version of this manuscript) :
— Sequence 4 – Polymorphic reification of the perceptual organs of an artefacted participant
— Sequence 5 – Assimilation of a subject to its artefact in a remediation proposal
— Sequence 6 – "Mise en abyme" of responsibility for the mobility of an artefacted participant when being asked to move the robot

Our analysis revealed a dual process of personification and reification at work in polyartefacted technobodily mediation. On the one hand, a vocal-gestural attribution of artefactual characteristics to the living subject by others – reification – and on the other, the vocal-gestural attribution of human characteristics to the subject's artefact – personification. The first movement, reification, is introduced into the interaction when the other prompts the artefact to take action, thereby identifying the artefact, whether intentionally or unintentionally, with the subject piloting it. In the second movement, personification, when the subject acts upon the artefact, the latter retroacts, and this retroaction perceived by the other is assimilated to human activity. The artefact perceived to be the subject of the action is attributed an intentionality, an agency of its own.

Moreover, the dual process of reification and personification seems to be expressed in a differentiated apprehension of matter. In the case of the reification of the animate, there is an effect of "materialisation" : a process that involves "using a material in order to give form to an abstraction" (Chatonsky 2015). This involves "instrumentalising matter under the authority of a conceptual enterprise" and its visual presentation aims to "translate digital data into some sort of form (image, sound, etc.)" (Chatonsky 2015), in response to a desire to make an abstraction sensible.

In the case of the "materiality" effect, here in the situation of the personification of the artefact, we need to conceive of matter as given and observe the networks woven by it (Chatonsky 2015).

In this dual process, the artefact acquires the form of a *persona* in the anthropological sense of the term : namely, the potential of everything, whether an object or a human being, to affirm a singular presence. This *persona* is enacted in a borderline presence : a sort of ambiguous presence that goes through varying degrees of intensity, from the most material to the most invisible.

Enacting an interworld

Interactants' hybrid presence crosses physical spaces and communication media via multimodal and multisemiotic actions undertaken by subjects, their corporeality and their artefacts. They draw on technobodily resources at their disposal, in order to preserve communication despite the multiple space-time frameworks. These technobodily resources are employed to flag mediation incidents (demediation), as well as to try to resolve them (remediation) and to achieve a state of media transparency (immediation). To this end, the subjects coordinate and cooperate among themselves and with the artefacts, both explicitly and implicitly, by embodying instances such as sentinels who flag mediation incidents, procurators who repair problems in the system of mediation, and witnesses who participate in the interactional event without intervening in the mediation process. Gestures are thus shared. There is an extension of the corporeal schema through the artefacts and the other subjects involved in the interaction and in the extended presence of each of the participants. Intersubjectivity is introduced into the corporeal schema that is extended to the other, and a form of transsubjectivity is enacted insofar as it goes beyond and cuts across technology and distance. The bodies become one, in order to interact in a complex technobodily network.

The transsubjective gesture and its action form part of a chain of distributed agency. Each of the interactants has the opportunity to contribute to the preservation of communication by way of any significant gesture, no matter how small. The communicative affordances and the positioning of the bodies and the artefacts in space entail that the subjects have to cooperate, since they cannot individually undertake the complex and reticular physical-digital mediation. The extended presence exists in the form of a flow running across subjects and artefacts. The gesture is constituted within a chain : It is initiated by some, and continued and completed by others, whether subjects or *tekhnê*. Distributed agency ensures an enlarged field of action.

Thus, every operation of percepaction is the result of a subject-artefact-other hybridisation, which gives rise to both the personification of the artefact and the reification of the animate. Indeed, corporeality is artefacted and artefacts are embodied ; there is intercorporeality in this percepactive extension.

If the body of the subject and that of the other form a single intercorporeality, objects are not left out and participate in this network of intersubjective perception to the extent that "our organs of perception are found both inside and outside, they are also to be included among the things through which we gain access to a specific dimension of a being's radiation" (Penayo 2016, 85).

Screen presence is thus the result of the multisemiotic, multimodal and sensory expression of artefacted subjects and involves the flesh and its extensions. The subjects are sentient beings who co-construct themselves in interaction by equipping themselves with technologies that allow them to overcome physical distance and to manifest themselves in multiple and reticular spatio-corporeal configurations. The subjects thus make themselves present to each other by way of an artefacted intercorporeality that enacts a world they share in common : an "interworld" (Merleau-Ponty 1964, 317).

References

Banks, Marcus, and Howard Morphy, eds. 1997. *Rethinking Visual Anthropology*. New Haven : Yale University Press.

Butler, Judith. 2002. *La Vie Psychique Du Pouvoir : L'assujettissement En Théories*. Translated by Brice Matthieussent. Paris : L. Scheer.

Casilli, Antonio. 2009. "Culture Numérique : L'adieu Au Corps n'a Jamais Eu Lieu." *Revue Esprit* 353 (March) : 151–53. Online.

———. 2012. "Être Présent En Ligne : Culture Et Structure Des Réseaux Sociaux d'Internet." *Idées Économiques Et Sociales* 3 (169) : 16–29. Online.

Chatonsky, Grégory. 2015. "Entre Matérialisation Numérique Et Matérialité Post-Digitale." Online.

Cosnier, Jacques. 2004. "Le Corps Et l'interaction (Empathie Et Analyseur Corporel)." Texte de communication Société Française de Psychologie. Online.

De Fornel, Michel. 2013. "Pour Une Approche Contextuelle Et Dynamique de l'agentivité." *Ateliers d'anthropologie* 2 (39) : 1–8. Online.

Dion, Delphine. 2007. "Les Apports de l'anthropologie Visuelle à l'étude Des Comportements de Consommation." *Recherche Et Applications En Marketing (French Edition)* 22 (1) : 61–78. Online.

Flichy, Patrice. 2009. "Le Corps Dans l'espace Numérique." *Revue Esprit* Mars/avril (3) : 163–74. Online.

Frias, Anibal. 2004. "Esthétique Ordinaire Et Chats : Ordinateur, Corporéité Et Expression Codifiée Des Affects." *Techniques & Culture. Revue Semestrielle d'anthropologie Des Techniques*, no. 42 (April) : 1–22. Online.

Goffman, Erving. 1973. *La Présentation de Soi*. La Mise En Scène de La Vie Quotidienne 1. Paris : Les Éditions de Minuit. Online.

Heidegger, Martin. 1985. *Les Problèmes Fondamentaux de La Phénoménologie*. Edited by Friedrich-Wilhelm von Herrmann. Translated by Jean-François Courtine. Paris : Gallimard.

Husserl, Edmund. 1929. *Méditations Cartésiennes Introduction à La Phénoménologie*. Translated by Gabrielle Peiffer and Emmanuel Levinas. Paris : J. Vrin.

Kerbrat-Orecchioni, Catherine. 2010. "Pour Une Analyse Multimodale Des Interactions Orales. L'expression Des Émotions Dans Les Débats Politiques Télévisuels." *Cadernos de Letras Da UFF* 40 : 17–45. Online.

Lamy, Marie-Noëlle. 2010. "Apprentissage Des Langues Médié Par Ordinateur : Discours Critiques Sur l'outil." *Le Français Dans Le Monde* 48 : 135–49. Online.

Le Breton, David. 2001. "La Délivrance Du Corps. Internet Ou Le Monde Sans Mal." *Revue Des Sciences Sociales* 28, nouve@ux mondes ? 20–26.

Maingueneau, Dominique. 1996. *Les Termes Clés de l'analyse Du Discours*. Paris : Éditions du Seuil.

Merleau-Ponty, Maurice. 1945. *Phénoménologie de La Perception*. Paris : Gallimard.

———. 1960. *Signes*. Paris : Gallimard. Online.

———. 1964. *Le Visible Et l'invisible*. Paris : Gallimard.

Mondada, Lorenza. 2008. "Using Video for a Sequential and Multimodal Analysis of Social Interaction : Videotaping Institutional Telephone Calls." *Forum Qualitative Sozialforschung / Forum : Qualitative Social Research* Vol 9 (3) : 1–35. Online.

Nadel, Jacqueline, and Jean Decety. 2006. "Résonnance Et Agentivité." *Cerveau Et Psycho* 13 : 50–53. Online.

Peirce, Charles. 1960. *Elements of Logic*. Collected Papers of Charles Sanders Peirce. Cambridge : Harvard University Press.

Penayo, José Duarte. 2016. "L'institution d'autrui Chez Merleau-Ponty : Vers Une Intercorporéité Expressive." Mémoire de Philosophie, Université Paris 1 Sorbonne. Online.

Pink, Sarah. 2007. *Doing Visual Ethnography : Images, Media, and Representation in Research*. 2nd ed. London ; Thousand Oaks, Calif : Sage Publications.

Ruby, Jay. 2000. *Picturing Culture : Explorations of Film & Anthropology*. Chicago : University of Chicago Press. Online.

Tisseron, Serge, Benoît Virole, Philippe Givre, Frédéric Tordo, Mathieu Triclot, and Yann Leroux. 2013. *Subjectivation Et Empathie Dans Les Mondes Numériques*. Paris : Dunod. Online.

Traverso, Véronique. 2012. "Longues Séquences Dans l'interaction : Ordre de l'activité, Cadres Participatifs Et Temporalités." *Langue Francaise* n°175 (3) : 53–73. Online.

Vial, Stéphane. 2013. *L'être Et l'écran : Comment Le Numérique Change La Perception*. Hors Collection. Paris : Presses universitaires de France. Online.

Weissberg, Jean-Louis. 2002. "Respirations de La Cyberculture." *Le Telemaque* 2 (22) : 7–12. Online.

New norms of politeness in digital contexts

Amélie Bouquain
Tatiana Codreanu
Christelle Combe

The aim of this chapter is to redefine politeness – a linguistic, semiotic and cultural concept – in a multimodal and polyartefactual communication context. In this complex interactional situation, different instances (determined by the status in the group or by the communication tools) and presence indicators (from physical to artefactual and interactional presence) have been analysed. In order to highlight participants' behaviour and acts of politeness, we used a multidisciplinary theoretical framework. This chapter addresses the following question : to what extent does the polyartefactual communication context affect the rituals of politeness ? It aims to document the group's evolution in terms of interpersonal relationships' regulations from the first to the last session. It also proposes, in the manner of H. Paul Grice's (1979) and Dan Sperber's (1989) maxims, a redefinition of new "rules" of politeness linked to the artefacted context.

Theoretical framework

Based on Erving Goffman's microsociology (1974), Penelope Brown and Stephen C. Levinson's (1978) theory of politeness adopts "face-saving" as a model while Jonathan Culpeper (1996) opts for "face-attack" as a model of impoliteness.
In order to study politeness in a polyartefactual context, we selected the following concepts.

Face-threatening and face-flattering acts

"Face" is "the positive social value that a person actually claims through the course of action that others assume they have taken in a particular contact" (Goffman 1974, 9, our translation) and "figuration" is "an act a person does to ensure that their actions do not cause anyone (including themselves) to lose face" (1974, 15, our translation). In order to study politeness, it is therefore necessary to observe *Face Threatening Acts* (FTA) or *Face Flattering Acts* (FFA) (Kerbrat-Orecchioni 1996), while taking into account the contextual aspects (Kerbrat-Orecchioni 2002). In our study, we focused on the polyartefactual context, precisely postulating that the same statement can be valid for a FTA in a given context, and for a FFA in another context, and vice versa.

Politeness rituals

Kerbrat-Orecchioni proposes the following definition of politeness rituals :

> [These] are regulated practices, which are reproduced more or less identically in identical situations... Ritual forms are poor in informational content, but rich in relational meaning. The absence of an expected ritual is seen as a threatening symptom of a tear in the social fabric, the consequences of which can be disastrous (2002, 512).

Thus, speech acts in the context of face-to-face interactions during the doctoral seminars follow a certain more or less codified ritual.

Terms of address

The terms of address, which are composed of pronominal forms, usually of the second person, and nominal forms of address (NFA) that designate and name the main addressee (Kerbrat-Orecchioni 2010), depending on the kind of interaction in which they occur, play a particular role : a role in the organisation and turn-taking, a role in the selection of the addressee and turn-taking, a role in strengthening the interlocutory link and the speech act and finally a role in relation to the interpersonal relationship (Kerbrat-Orecchioni 2010). Their role is also essential in conversational openings and closings.

The notion of cooperation

The notion of cooperation, which is seen in the context of figuration by Goffman, is also studied in evolutionary biology. According to Martin A. Nowak (2006a; 2006b), in a group, one can distinguish three types of behaviour: individuals who cooperate (cooperators and super-cooperators), individuals who decide to stay out of cooperation (defectors) and individuals who observe other agents' behaviors with respect to acts of cooperation and defection (discriminators). Nowak emphasises the cost associated with cooperative behaviour (by providing a benefit to other individuals).

The status of the participants

The polyartefactual doctoral seminar forms in Goffman's sense, a team, that is :

> a set of people whose very close cooperation is essential to maintain a given definition of the situation. It is a group that is related, not to a social structure or social organisation, but rather to an interaction or series of interactions in which the proper definition of the situation is maintained (Goffman 1973, 102).

The members of a team are interdependent and seek to give the representation expected by the audience.
Based on the notion of a dynamic participatory framework (Goffman 1987) and the analytical inputs of evolutionary biology, we distinguished the following statuses :

— Passive and active interlocutory status that can change during the interaction.

— Ratified (or authorised) participants who are officially part of the conversational group, as evidenced above all by the physical "arrangement" of this group, and the non-verbal behaviour of its members (distance and proxemic organisation, postural configurations, gaze network, vocal intensity) (Kerbrat-Orecchioni 2010, 86),

— Unratified participants (spectators) – they are excluded in principle from the interaction and have a spectator status,

— Participants who are listening and who are in the field of view of the ratified participants,

— Intruders, and those who are not in the field of view of the ratified participants,

— Discriminators (Nowak 2006a; 2006b) – ratified, or unratified participants, in the field of view or outside the field of view, attributing value in relation to the way the interactions are taking place or have taken place. Discriminators observe other participants' behaviours in order to update their opinions about the other participants' reputations.

In order to define the rituals of politeness in the context of the doctoral seminar, this chapter will answer the following research questions :

— What forms of address were used ? (diachronic perspective)

— What is a threatening act in a polyartefactual context ?

— What is a cooperative act in a polyartefactual context ?

— What new rules of politeness should be implemented in this context ?

Analysis and results

Nominal forms of address : diachronic evolution

In this section, we will analyse the nominal forms used to address or designate the participants who, in order to participate remotely in the doctoral seminar, had to use an artefact (Adobe Connect, Beam or Kubi). Our analysis is diachronic from the first to the last session of the corpus of study.

In this polyartefactual context, it is necessary to take into account the characteristics of the artefacts used, but also the different "spheres of interaction [36]" that are inherent to them.

As the system was set up, with participants connected *via* the Beam and Kubi robots, Adobe Connect and the face-to-face group, meant that there could technically only be synchronous oral interactions (*intra* sphere of interaction). However, all participants had the possibility to connect to Adobe Connect as well – those in the face-to-face group as well as those using Beam and Kubi – allowing for synchronous written exchanges through Adobe Connect chat (*inter* sphere of interaction).

During the doctoral seminars, all participants referred to each other by their first names. Informal language was used between permanent members and the use of "*vous*" (you, plural) was related to addressing the group and the guest

---

36. By "sphere of interaction", we mean the space open to interactions that the artefact allows. Interactions can therefore take place within this space and be characterised as *inter* or *intra* when the interactions take place in spaces of intersection between different spheres (when using several artefacts), for example a computer connected to the video-conferencing software is used for a whole face-to-face group, including the artefacts present in the room, such as Beam and Kubi remote presence robots.

speakers (formal). Our analysis focuses on the NFA used by face-to-face participants to refer to remote participants. The analysis of the corpus of study at the macro level allows us to define three levels of perception and representation corresponding to membership categorisation devices (Sacks 1992). These levels influenced the designation of remote participants by face-to-face participants, and in particular by the participant who has the leadership role in the seminar :

— Group categorisation – the group effect of remote participants, relative to the group of individuals,
— Artefactual categorisation – an artefact used to monitor the seminar remotely, relative to the object,
— Individual categorisation – identity of the remote participant, relative to the individual.

This categorisation demonstrated by our analysis shows a perception ranging from the general to the individual level and thus a graduation in the representation of the group and of the remote participants linked to the effects of presence. We conducted our analysis at the micro level through these three categorisations.

To do so, we recorded and analysed the NFA used in each session and noted the changes we observed between the first and last sessions.

	Group cat.	Artefactual cat.	Individual cat.
Session 1	X	X	X
Session 2	X	X	X
Session 3	X		X
Session 4			X
Session 5			X

Session 1

From the very first session, in addressing others, we observe different terms of address between face-to-face and remote participants, as if beyond the different artefacts used by the remote participants, there were two spaces that coexisted through group effects : a face-to-face group and a remote group.

Session 2

Session 2 is characterised by the presence of guest speakers. It should be noted, however, that on three occasions the first names of the participants were used directly to address them, which constitutes a change in the terms of address.

Session 3 – Parts 1 and 2

The classification and division into three categorisations of the NFA used in Session 3 shows the disappearance of the artefactual categorisation, i.e., the designation of the participants by the name of the artefact used, but also a more pronounced tendency towards individual categorisation, i.e., the use of terms of address relating to the individual ("Amélie, Tatiana", "the remote people").

From this session onwards, we noted a change in the NFA used to address the remote participants, in this case the use of their first names to address them, particularly by Christine.

Session 4

In Session 4, only terms relating to people were used ("Christelle would like to talk", "Christelle, you…", "Ah, you didn't turn your mic on"); the participants stopped using terms relating to the representation of the remote group (group categorisation) and to the artefacts used (artefactual categorisation).

Session 5 – Parts 1 and 2

During Session 5, only the first names of the remote participants were used to refer to them, thus the group and artefactual categorisations changed, which confirmed a real evolution between Session 1 and Session 5, and this despite the
different artefacts used, the number of participants connected remotely and the typology of the participants (member
of the research group or guest speaker).

Threatening acts and repair processes

In this section, we study different face-threatening acts in
this polyartefactual context, and the face-repairing strategies implemented by the participants.

Firstly, we studied the case of a "misunderstanding". The
scene took place during Session 2, when the moderator
welcomed two guest speakers to the seminar for the first
time. The conference took place with very poor sound
quality for the participants on Adobe Connect. Only one
Adobe Connect microphone was activated on one of the
computers in the seminar room, which was too far away
from the guest speakers.

Christelle's will to participate and be present despite technical difficulties was manifested in her abrupt speech within
an engaged conversation, which in this case proves to be a
FTA for the face of the person being interrupted, but also
for the person committing the FTA. On both sides there
were restorative processes and group cohesion was rebuilt
around the incident.

Another form of FTA observed during the polyartefactual
seminar is linked to hyperpoliteness.

These various terms of address also proved to be a FTA for
different participants when they did not intend to speak,
either because they had nothing relevant to say on the subject, or because they could not hear properly for technical

reasons, or because they do not necessarily felt competent on the subject to speak in front of the entire group.

Cooperative acts as flattering acts

To illustrate the links we make between cooperative acts and face-flattering acts, we have analysed Session 4 in detail.

The interaction analysis shows that cooperative acts can be equated with acts of politeness. Nevertheless, cooperative participants did not necessarily impose a strategy of cooperation during the doctoral seminar. Groups were formed and split by the constraint of size, positioning in the room, strategies for occupying chairs, and the search for a place that optimised sound and visual reception. The selection model was thus based on the notion of technical optimum. Cooperation was precarious and cooperative behaviours did not emerge in a stable way either for participants in the room or for participants at a distance. Cooperative groups could be overwhelmed by non-cooperative choices. However, stable behaviours did occur when participants cooperate around data recording and knowledge sharing.

The acts of cooperation analysis highlight the impact of the 3D design of the room that structures the interactional environment. This corporeality was not the same for a 2D image projected on a wall which deprived the participants of a 3D physical form on Adobe Connect. We could then observe that the design of the initial experience (the seminar room, the physical configuration and the choice of artefacts) formed a perceptual horizon that affected the interactions between the seminar participants. The difficulties linked to the projected image of Adobe Connect and to the functionalities of the platform (limited visibility for people in the room) added a degree of interactional complexity that required a degree of learning from participants of the new "body", the 2D projected image. While the movement of the 3D bodies in the room easily attracted the attention of the participants present in the physical space of the seminar room, the Adobe Connect image projected on the wall required an additional effort for the interactions in progress (looking up, a passive artefact that was easily forgotten in the absence of any sign of an anatomical and physical reality). Thus, the positioning and nature of the various artefacts in the physical space of the seminar room played a considerable role.

New "maxims"

In a polyartefacted context, interaction rites must therefore be put in place, and learning about a new "hybrid interaction culture" is thus indispensable. We propose the following maxims for a polyartefactual seminar in the manner of Grice :

— Maxim of interactional opening – Log in 15 minutes before the interactions commence, enter the "interactional space" (Ibnelkaïd 2015).

— Participants maxim – Introduce all the participants by name, including those who are invisible on the screens (or off camera).

— Platform maxim – Connect all participants to the same platform with the same rights and ask them to individually manage their camera and audio (microphone and sound).

— Addressing maxim – Use the person's name or surname when addressing them, position yourself facing the robot or facing the camera on the interactive multimodal platform, adjust your gaze.

— Maxim of communication – When a channel is not working (audio, mic, camera), remember to use the other channels (chat, camera, message). Keep an eye on each space regularly, remember to turn off your microphone when you are not speaking.

— Silence maxim – Learn to tolerate silence and sometimes long pauses.
— Maxim of movement – Ask the artefact user's permission before moving or adjusting an artefact.
— Maxim of interactional closing – Close the interaction with all the participants and across all the artefacts; do not disconnect abruptly.

The diachronic analysis of the NFAs used by the face-to-face
participants to address or designate the remote participants
showed that over a period of six months there was a strong
attenuation of the group effect (group categorisation) and
an evolution of the terms used, from designating mainly
the artefact (artefactual categorisation) to addressing participants by their first name, and thus a disappearance of two
categorisations linked to the effects of presence in favour of
the individual categorisation.

The micro qualitative analysis of various FTA and face-
repairing strategies shows that these are often related to the
effect of the medium or a technical malfunction, and that it
is important for different participants to master not only the
artefact they are using, but also the one their interlocutor
is using. To put it more simply, ideally, all the participants
would have had practice using all the artefacts to create the
conditions for the empathy necessary for a satisfactory interaction.

A group effect will always be able to operate at the level
of the co-operators and thus compensate for the potential shortcomings of other participants. The design study
of rooms where interactions using artefacts take place can
show how acts of politeness and cooperation can be influenced by the architecture and design of the space itself.
The strategy of occupying a space is strongly linked to the
search for technical optimum, and the absence of an equi-

librium has a direct influence on acts of politeness and co-operation.

References

Brown, Penelope, and Stephen C. Levinson. 1978. "Universals in Language Usage : Politeness Phenomena." In *Questions and Politeness : Strategies in Social Interaction*, edited by Esther N.Goody, 56–311. Ann Arbor, Michigan : Cambridge University Press.

Culpeper, Jonathan. 1996. "Towards an Anatomy of Impoliteness." *Journal of Pragmatics* 25 (3) : 349–67. Online.

Goffman, Erving. 1973. *La Présentation de Soi*. La Mise En Scène de La Vie Quotidienne 1. Paris : Les Éditions de Minuit. Online.

———. 1974. *Les Rites d'interaction*. Paris : Les Éditions de Minuit. Online.

———. 1987. *Façons de Parler*. Paris : Les Éditions de Minuit. Online.

Grice, H. Paul. 1979. "Logique Et Conversation." *Communications* 30 (1) : 57–72. Online.

Ibnelkaïd, Samira. 2015. "Scénographie d'une Ouverture d'interaction Vidéo." *Réseaux* 6 (194) : 125–68. Online.

Kerbrat-Orecchioni, Catherine. 1996. *La Conversation*. Mémo Lettres Sciences Sociales 25. Paris : Éditions du Seuil.

———. 2002. "Politesse En Deçà Des Pyrénées, Impolitesse Au-Delà : Retour Sur La Question de l'universalité de La (Théorie de La) Politesse." *Marges Linguistiques* 2.

———. 2010. "Pour Une Approche Contrastive Des Formes Nominales d'adresse." *Journal of French Language Studies* 20 (1) : 3–15. Online.

Nowak, Martin A. 2006a. *Evolutionary Dynamics : Exploring the Equations of Life*. Cambridge, Mass : Belknap Press of Harvard University Press.

———. 2006b. "Five Rules for the Evolution of Cooperation." *Science (New York, N.y.)* 314 (5805) : 1560–63. Online.

Sacks, Harvey. 1992. *Lectures on Conversation*. Edited by Gail
Jefferson. Oxford, UK : Blackwell.

Sperber, Dan, and Deirdre Wilson. 1989. *La Pertinence :
Communication Et Cognition*. Paris : Les Éditions de Minuit. Online.

Autonomy and artefactual presence in a polyartefacted seminar

Amélie Bouquain
Christelle Combe
Joséphine Rémon

As presented in the introduction of this book, three telepresence devices were used in the seminar : the telepresence robots Beam and Kubi as well as the web conferencing software program Adobe Connect. In this chapter, in the light of work in interactive multimodal communication and more specifically in robot-mediated communication (Herring 2013 ; Takayama and Go 2012 ; Takayama and Harris 2013 ; Neustaedter et al. 2016 ; Sirkin et al. 2011 ; Gaver 1992), we interrogate the notion of artefactual presence through a comparative study of the affordances of these devices. We ask how the effects of presence related to each device define an artefactual presence or an interactional presence, depending on the interactional co-construction implemented by the participants. To what extent do effects of presence vary according to the artefact or a particular device and in the co-construction of its use by the different members ? Our study is based on interviews with participants (Amélie, Jean-François, Samira, Christelle) which we cross-reference with the analysis of certain critical moments in the video corpus of the sessions.

Theoretical framework

Several studies in multimodal communication and human-computer communication have demonstrated the characteristics of the different telepresence devices used and their effects on communication.

The researchers point to parameters such as rotation or field of view, but also to characteristics of the mediated space (within which the interaction takes place), such as the lack of symmetry in the transmission and reception of sound and image between the different participants.

An approach focused on interaction and not on geographical location

In studies on meetings involving co-located and remotely located participants, the geographical location is often emphasised. The meeting with the co-located participants is defined as a "hub" while the remote location, present in the form of a "proxy" or artefact enabling the remote participant to participate (screen, video camera, speaker, microphone), is a "satellite" (Sirkin et al. 2011, 163). This "hub/satellite" view thus focuses on the technical device and not on the experience of the interaction.

In our study, in contrast, we do not consider one place as the "hub" and another as a "satellite". This is because there were sometimes fewer participants in the seminar room than online, and because there were different "satellite locations" (as opposed to a single satellite individual in the case of Sirkin et al.). Thus, in order to correspond to the actual lived experience, the present/remote dualism must be overcome in favour of an approach centred on interaction and not on geographical location.

Engagement and mobility

Other researchers have studied telepresence devices from the perspective of interactional engagement and movement effects. Herring (2013, 1), for example, points to difficulties with Adobe Connect-type devices, including sound and visualisation issues, participant fatigue, difficulty in feeling engaged in the interaction, and frustrations with speaking difficulties :

> However, currently popular teleconferencing tools (e.g., Skype, Adobe) are limited in various respects. Even when video is added to audio communication, remote participants often cannot see or hear everyone at the remote location, may feel disengaged and fa-

tigued (because more effort is required to pay attention), and may experience interactional frustration due to difficulty getting the floor and identifying who is speaking (e.g., Egido 1990; Sirkin et al. 2011).

This difficulty in feeling engaged is partly due to the lack of possibility of movement. According to Gaver (1992, 21), the possibility of exploring the environment through movement is not a constitutive characteristic of mediated spaces since the cameras and microphones are fixed and controlled by the people on site. According to the author, being online feels more like watching television than having control over a perceptual exploration.

Conversely, "kinetic proxies" (which can be set in motion, such as the Beam or Kubi) allow for a hybrid approach (Sirkin et al. 2011, 166) by combining motion and video image, as opposed to a robot which would be a simple avatar of the remote person. The artefact thus represents the remote participant and reminds the group of their presence through movement or rotation. According to the study led by Sirkin et al., the quality of conversational engagement is higher when motion is possible :

> The motorized action brought the remote person to life. Hub participants were able to perceive the satellite's attention in motion through the swivelling of the display (2011, 176).

Compared to a video-conferencing device, the Kubi's rotational mobility creates an additional effect of presence (Herring 2013, 3). In addition to its small size, its screen can be rotated to follow the conversation. However, the Kubi cannot be entirely piloted in the same way as the Beam (Herring 2013, 3) since it has to be carried from one place to another by a human agent.

Sirkin et al. (2011) have also revealed undesirable effects of motion. Rotation can be interpreted as a disruption, and as an interruption for the remote participant who must operate this rotation. When the participant rotates the device to face an interlocutor, it can be perceived as though they are "turning their back" on other participants :

> screen motion towards one person is more akin to turning one's back (rather than one's head) towards someone else (Sirkin et al. 2011, 164).

Another difficulty is that head movements and rotational movements of artefacts are not always interpreted in the same way, as participants seek to attribute intelligibility to these movements, even though some may be mere incidents lacking any communicative purpose.

We study these various movement effects in our context, and analyse below how they combine with characteristics of autonomy (see "Analysis and results").

Disrupted reciprocity of perceptions in the mediated space

In the field of human-computer interaction, Gaver (1992, 17) compares the affordances of an unmediated situation with a media space defined as a space created by "computer-controllable networks of audio and video equipment used to support synchronous collaboration". He identifies the following characteristics of the latter space : distant collaboration, restricted field of vision, impossible detailed inspection, limited peripheral awareness, biased sound transmission, limited perceptual exploration, and discontinuity of spaces that make speech turns and communicative behaviours more difficult. These characteristics apply to the situation we analyse in this study.

Media spaces are also characterised by anisotropy, i.e., the non-reciprocity of perceptions in the mediated space[37], in

---

37. See chapter "Attentional affordances in an instrumented seminar".

contrast to air (i.e., face-to-face communication). This term comes from physics and is applied when the properties of an object vary according to direction. As Gaver (1992, 23) explains, air is isotropic and allows for reciprocity of perceptions [38] :

> Air is isotropic with respect to light and – unless it is moving – with respect to sound as well. This means that air affords reciprocal communication, that people can predict what their partners will see and hear by what they themselves see and hear.

Screen mediation therefore disrupts this reciprocity by making the exchanges anisotropic. This is reflected, for example, in the difficulty for participants in the seminar room to know precisely what a remote participant is looking at. Sirkin et al. (2011) point out the importance for the remote participant to have an broad view of a space, so as to be able to follow which attentional foci [39] are being activated. Many parameters may be unknown to the participants in the seminar room (Sirkin et al. 2011, 164) : this is the case, for example, of the angle of view of the remote participant's camera or the size of their computer screen. Furthermore, according to these authors, the "TV presenter effect" makes face-to-face participants feel as though they are all being looked at simultaneously if the satellite is looking at the camera, or all neglected if it looks away. They also note the "skip-over effect", whereby the remote participant tends to be neglected despite the presence of the face-to-face artefact that represents them.

At the end of this brief literature review, we note that the complexity of the situation is due in particular to the ani-

---

38. See chapter "Attentional affordances in an instrumented seminar".

39. See chapter "Attentional affordances in an instrumented seminar".

sotropy of the mediated space, as well as to the affordances of the telepresence devices used, depending on the possibilities of movement or rotation, but also depending on the way these movements happen and are interpreted by the participants. On the basis of these elements, we can now analyse the interactional characteristics of our corpus and the effects of presence they generate.

Analysis and results

Remote communication devices present different potentialities of movement, vision and hearing, which have impact in terms of presence effects, around issues of transmission/reception, and visibility/invisibility or presence/absence : one can be present and invisible to others or visible and absent. These effects of presence define an artefactual presence or an interactional presence, depending on the interactional co-construction implemented by the participants. We define artefactual presence as the presence of the object with a reduced possibility of interaction, as opposed to interactional presence which allows an individual to take their place in the interaction without hindrance. As we will see below, it is mainly the issues of autonomy of movement and visual and sound adjustment that determine the objectal or interactional status of the pilot and her artefact. These presence effects bring into play conviviality, stealth [40], reactions to solicitation or orders as well as temporality (beginning/end).

Autonomy of rotation and movement

Rotations and movements are characterised by parameters of autonomy : are movements possible or impossible, auto-

---

40. We mean stealth in the military sense of being designed to avoid detection by using a variety of technologies that reduce signature.

nomously driven or dependent on others? The movement must also be considered in terms of the starting position : was this chosen by the user? Additionally, is the movement translational and/or rotational (is it a head or artefact rotation; slow or fast rotation; discreet or noisy rotation)? A distinction will therefore be made between movement in production and the effect of movement in reception.

Movement range of the Beam

Our experimentation showed us that the Beam offered its user only a relative autonomy of movement.
In Session 2, we find another illustration of the limitations of the Beam's possibilities, when the presence of the artefact seems to be spatially related to group presence.
When the speakers move their table to get closer to the microphone that is transmitting the sound to the remote participants, Amélie, the Beam user, has situated the Beam between this table and the tables behind her, where the participants in Lyon are seated.
Even if she experiences this change of configuration as uncomfortable, she cannot move because she is hampered by the tables which limit her movements and make it difficult to move to another part of the room :

> It's true that, wow, when they came closer, I felt that the normal distance, the interpersonal distance between people, was completely disrespected, they were practically up against me […] it wasn't very comfortable.

In this case, the comfort of the remote person is replaced by that of the participants in the seminar room.
In other cases, the Beam pilot can sometimes exercise autonomy in piloting the artefact, as we explain now.

Effect of presence of the Beam's autonomous piloting

In Session 3 (group work), we see an example of the effect of presence of the Beam's movement, which is also commented on by the pilot in an interview.

During the group discussion, the Beam starts to rotate slightly on its wheels and then suddenly moves towards the centre of the room. Christine exclaims, "Oh, she scared me!" and Morgane, putting her hand over her heart, says "Oh my goodness!" However, the interruption does not last more than 5 seconds.

From our analyses, artefactual or interactional presence depends on perception by others as much as oneself. In an anisotropic mediated space, participants rely as much on the perception of others as on their own perception in an attempt to reconstruct a comprehensive perception and allow the interaction to function.

Artefactual presence of the Kubi

Our analyses identify different situations in which the presence of the artefact pilot is reduced to artefactual presence. Artefactual presence can take over, for example, through a request for permission to move the artefact by someone else. This request points to a potential interactional presence, even if sometimes the artefact is rotated even though the pilot has not responded to a request for permission.

So although the Kubi does have a certain rotational autonomy, it still needs to be mastered and must correspond to the configuration at a given moment and in a given space. In some cases, such as above, artefactual presence is brought to the fore.

Audio-visual autonomy

In addition to the effects of movement, the angle of vision is also a determining parameter. As a whole, the artefactual communication situation at stake is complex. Firstly, the Kubi user has to choose a setting that allows her to adjust the view on the computer screen. Secondly, the camera within the seminar room that transmits the image to Adobe Connect must also be adjusted to produce suitable visual content. The combination of these two actions allows the Kubi user to feel like they are part of the situation. While face-to-face participants can visually scan a space, remote artefact participants may not see the technical solutions deployed in the room, for example, or certain actions, such as drawing on the board. For the purposes of this paper, we distinguish between audio-visual autonomy and autonomy of movement, but audio-visual perception and autonomous or provoked movement are of course interdependent, because if the angle of vision is a barrier to interactional felicity, then remediation involves positional adjustment, either autonomous or assisted.

Limitations in the field of vision and rotation of the Kubi

The Kubi's field of vision is limited and must be set by the pilot, which has implications in terms of artefactual presence. Interactional presence implies at times an artefactual presence; in order to *be* or *become present*, one has to transiently pass through moments of artefactual presence, for instance, when one is assisted by another participant and is momentarily recategorised, not as a pilot, but as an object.

Adjusting the Kubi's field of vision

The Kubi's limited field of vision deprives the pilot of some of the interactions that take place in Lyon.

Adjustment of the camera's field of vision in the seminar room

The Kubi pilot depends on the help of the participants in Lyon to adjust her angle of vision, which moderates her interactional power. In contrast, the Beam pilot can adjust her field of view autonomously. She has greater agency in this respect.

The "back" of the Beam

Even though the Beam pilot can move the device autonomously, she still has a limited field of vision of what is happening behind the artefact. Our analysis of the video demonstrates this limitation, and the Beam pilot confirms it in an interview.

The choices made about the issues of transmission and reception, such as adapting the Adobe Connect software for hybrid use (a group in a room/individuals in separate locations), had consequences for audio reception (e.g., participants on Adobe Connect could not hear participants in the room) or visual reception (e.g., participants in the room could not tell apart the silhouettes of participants on Adobe Connect.) who were against the light. These different types of perceptual (motion and audio-visual) autonomy influence the availability and participation regimes allowing the interaction to function.

Participatory autonomy

The technical choices and the potentialities of each device have an impact on participation. By participatory autonomy we mean the regulation initiated by the individual of their involvement in the interaction.

Issues of availability for being spoken to can appear according to whether the artefact allows a participant to participate in the interaction in reception or in transmission.

Difficulty in calling the Beam

The participants found it easier to address the Adobe Connect users than the Beam pilot. Morgane explains in an interview that she tried several times and through several channels (signs, chat, email, SMS) to contact Amélie, the Beam pilot, without success.

Difficulty in giving a strong visual signal when using the Kubi or Adobe Connect

The Kubi or Adobe Connect users also found it difficult to speak up. In the Kubi, unless you speak up and impose your voice, you cannot address the rest of the group.

In the Adobe Connect chat function it is equally difficult to send a strong signal.

More broadly, we can thus question whether participation in the interaction is subject to regimes that could be described as artefactual, in the sense that they are dependent on the artefact, or the telepresence device used.

The chat as a space for autonomous or relayed communication

Still from the point of view of participatory autonomy, we see in this section that the communication space of the chat is ambivalent, in that it sometimes allows participation in the overall interaction, not in an autonomous way but through the on-site participants, and sometimes generates a separate space for autonomous communication.

The remote participants using Adobe Connect all have access to the chat. Some participants in the room are also connected to Adobe Connect and use the chat, which is projected, but despite this, the content of the chat sometimes has to be relayed [41].

The social aspect of the chat is pointed out in interviews by various members of the team.

On the contrary, Amélie, the Beam pilot, indicates in an interview that it was difficult for her to access the communica-

---

41. See chapter "Attentional affordances in an instrumented seminar".

tion space created by the chat function (unless she manipulated both the Beam and Adobe Connect interfaces simultaneously). Jean-François and Samira both point out the compartmentalisation aspects of the chat.

The chat is sometimes a space for autonomous exchanges, whose participants no longer want to be part of the general group interaction.

Below we explore constraints or orders in terms of participation in the interaction from the point of view of autonomy and intention. These elements involve screen presence, the necessity of thinking about framing of one's own picture from the viewer's point of view, or hyper-exposure when speaking.

Over-ratification and over-exposure

Based on the concept of ratification (Goffman 1981), we analyse examples of what we call "over-ratification" : an exposed and undesirable ratification from the point of view of remote participants [42]; and of what we call "hyper-exposure", i.e., taking a conversational turn without wanting to.

Unwanted exposure sometimes occurs via an incidental audio hyper-exposure, which takes over a speech turn without the person intending to. For example, when the Beam user sneezes at home [43], due to the anisotropy of the mediated space, she does not realise that the sound effect is dramatically amplified in the room.

Voluntary hypo-exposure

The anisotropy of the mediated space (Gaver 1992, 234), i.e., the fact that the space has different characteristics de-

---

42. See chapter "New norms of politeness in digital contexts".

43. See chapters "New norms of politeness in digital contexts" and "Artefacted intercorporeality, between reification and personification".

pending on the orientation, makes it possible to spy on others, or to be artefactually present while being absent, or on the contrary to "arrive" unnoticed by the participants in the room.

The Beam's "zoom" function in particular can give the user a stealthy presence, unbeknownst to the other participants. But while the robot's movement creates an effect, its immobility is not synonymous with inactivity, even if the participants in the room do not realise it.

Generally speaking, affordances are negotiated by taking into account a set of parameters, such as the delayed adjustments of the Beam in this case.

We have seen through this study that the effect of presences linked to each device define an artefactual presence or an interactional presence, depending on the interactional co-construction implemented by the participants. The issues of autonomy of movement and visual and sound adjustment determine the objectal or interactional status of the user and the device they are using.

The duality between objectal and interactional status does not presume interactional felicity. Artefactual presence sometimes corresponds to the user's intention in that it allows discretion, just as interactional presence can then go against the user's intention in that it sometimes creates situations of over-ratification. Artefactual presence can be experienced against one's will (e.g., the Beam is moved during the break and when the pilot reconnects it has no cues) or can be taken advantage of (e.g., the Beam pilot uses the zoom function unobtrusively while the participants in the room are unaware that the pilot is connected, or the Beam is moved by others, which facilitates the interaction). Similarly, interactional presence can be experienced against one's will (e.g., the floor is explicitly given to participants online when they have nothing in particular to say at that

moment) or can be taken advantage of (e.g., when a request in the chat is relayed to the room verbally).
To conclude this analysis, we propose the following table to sum up these categories :

	Artefactual presence	Interactional presence
Against one's ratification will	Exemple : Being inappropriately moved by others	Example : Over-ratification
Taken advantage of	Example : Being moved by others with interactional intent	Example : chat contribution relayed orally in-situ

In addition to an analysis centred around the characteristics of the telepresence devices used, the regulations involving the regimes of autonomy are played out in the intentions of each person and their interpretation, which allow interactions to be co-constructed in a polyartefacted hybrid context, within an artefacted-interactional community.

References

Egido, Carmen. 1990. "Teleconferencing as a Technology to Support Cooperative Work : Its Possibilities and Limitations." In *Intellectual Teamwork : Social and Technological Foundations of Cooperative Work*, edited by Jolene Rae Galegher, Robert E. Kraut, and Carmen Egido, 351–71. Hillsdale, N.J : L. Erlbaum Associates.

Gaver, William W. 1992. "The Affordances of Media Spaces for Collaboration." *Proc. CSCW 1992, ACM Press*, 17–24. Online.

Goffman, Erving. 1981. *Forms of Talk*. University of Pennsylvania Publications in Conduct and Communication. Philadelphia : University of Pennsylvania Press. Online.

Herring, Susan C. 2013. "Telepresence Robots for Academics." *Proceedings of the American Society for Information Science and Technology* 50 (1) : 1–4. Online.

Neustaedter, Carman, Gina Venolia, Jason Procyk, and Dan Hawkins. 2016. "To Beam or Not to Beam : A Study of Remote Telepresence Attendance at an Academic Conference." In *Proceedings of the 19th ACM Conference on Computer-Supported Cooperative Work & Social Computing*, 417–30. ACM. Online.

Sirkin, David, Gina Venolia, John Tang, George Robertson, Taemie Kim, Kori Inkpen, Mara Sedlins, Bongshin Lee, and Mike Sinclair. 2011. "Motion and Attention in a Kinetic Videoconferencing Proxy." In *Human-Computer Interaction – INTERACT 2011*, edited by Pedro Campos, Nicholas Graham, Joaquim Jorge, Nuno Nunes, Philippe Palanque, and Marco Winckler, 162–80. Lecture Notes in Computer Science. Springer Berlin Heidelberg. Online.

Takayama, Leila, and Janet Go. 2012. "Mixing Metaphors in Mobile Remote Presence." In, 495–504. ACM. Online.

Takayama, Leila, and Helen Harris. 2013. "Presentation of (Telepresent) Self : On the Double-Edged Effects of Mirrors." In, 381–88. IEEE Press. Online.

Digital bugs and interactional failures in the service of a collective intelligence

Samira Ibnelkaïd
Caroline Vincent

The emergence of communication networks and interfaces has brought about a reconfiguration of individuals' modes of presence and modalities of interaction. Onscreen interactional experiences have led to the creation of new linguistic resources and of a renewed relationship to space and time, as well as to others and to oneself.

The reticular and diffracted aspect of these new forms of interaction entails the development of a new technobodily literacy. Individuals need to adapt to the conversational failures inherent to all social interaction (Kerbrat-Orecchioni 1990; Traverso 1999; Béal 2010) and the "technical bugs intrinsic to digital technologies" (Vial 2012). The versatility of digital matter (Vial 2012) and the fragility of social interaction (Kerbrat-Orecchioni 1996) show how much communication is co-constructed and based on cooperation. During their onscreen experience, individuals need to collaborate in order to initiate, maintain, preserve and repair the flow of communication, in particular, during critical episodes that are inevitable in polylogal, polyartefacted interactions.

This raises the question of the methods used by interactants to deal with these critical episodes. How does the group identify and overcome digital bugs and interactional failures during onscreen interactions, and how does it enacts a collective intelligence?

Our study started with an ethological description of a critical episode in which we observed the difficulties participants encounter in trying to make their activities accountable and the ethnomethods they develop to overcome these difficulties. This description was accompanied by a transdisciplinary synthesis of the results of the three main axis of our research : the study of attention from a communicational point of view, that of corporeality in a phenomenological approach, and that of politeness from an interactionist perspective. Finally, these new theoretical-analytical findings were linked to the discursive analysis of the final assessment questionnaires completed by participants, in particular, on the key points of their experience and their recommendations.

Failures and bugs : Incidents inherent to (onscreen) communication

Verbal interactions and their failures

Interactional felicity

During their interactions, individuals are constantly trying to understand their interlocutor and to make themselves understood by them. Participants employ a variety of multimodal and multisemiotic resources to maintain this intelligibility.

Interactional felicity thus consists in the speaker being able to express a thought, to make it understood or gain approbation for it, to share an opinion, etc. (Cosnier 1996). This felicity is determined by the answers to the speaker's four questions : Do you hear me ? Are you listening to me ? Do you understand me ? What do you think about it ? (Cosnier 1996).

Interactive bricolage

But this affective framing does not come into being without incidents. The constant search for interactional felicity regularly entails adjustments inasmuch as communication necessarily involves malfunctions. The interactionist approach defines an interactional malfunction as "a linguistic phenomenon that transgresses a rule of the ideal functioning of interaction" (Sandré 2009, 69). These malfunctions are interactional failures (Kerbrat-Orecchioni 1990; Traverso 1999).

These conversational incidents reveal the processes through which interactants engage in a cooperative process that seeks to prevent communication from coming to a full stop. It is thus clear that a social interaction rarely takes place without linguistic snags; failure is an intrinsic element of communication. What is important for participants is not simply trying to avoid failures, but, above all, learning to deal with them and to overcome them.

Digital technology and its bugs

The volatility of digital matter

When interactions take place through screens, participants also have to deal with incidents related to digital technology. Technology is itself a source of failures. As Stéphane Vial (2013, 213) explains, versatility is one of the intrinsic structural characteristics of digital phenomena, since "bugs are consubstantial with calculated matter" (2013, 213); a digital artefact "cannot live without bugs" (2013, 214). Although, software programs and algorithms were created by humans, they do not guarantee perfectly controllable functioning a priori.

Nonetheless, it is still difficult to understand and accept the element of the unknown and unpredictable that digital technology introduces into our communication and our experience of the world, in the sense that there is a paradox between the growing power of these tools and their permanent fragility. Their users expect these ultra-connected, high-performance devices to respond to their needs right away, and they thus become more and more intolerant of technical incidents or bugs. Inasmuch as this instability is intrinsic to digital equipment, we need to develop a digital literacy that includes education about digital versatility. We need to learn to live with bugs : to accept their effects and to circumvent the damage they cause (2013, 216).

The collective and its intelligence

Construction of membership

Well-functioning onscreen interactions are based on the participants' ability to make themselves visible and to make their productions and the activities in which they are situated intelligible. How social actors grasp the construction of intelligibility is at the heart of ethnomethodological research. This approach

> seeks to analyse the social world not as it is given, but rather as it is continually in the process of being made, continually emerging, as an orderly, intelligible and familiar objective reality (Quéré 1990, 75).

Harold Garfinkel (1967), the founder of ethnomethodology, defined it as an approach that

> analyzes everyday activities as members' methods for making those same activities visibly-rational-and-reportable-for-all-practical-purposes, i.e., "accountable", as organizations of commonplace everyday activities (1967, vii).

The concept underlying this whole approach, accountability, alludes to the fact that (re)cognisability, intelligibility and describability are essential properties of action (Mondada 2006, 117).
Participants in the interaction then have to share a natural language in common ; they draw on specific ethnomethods to organise their interaction. These shared ethnomethods form the basis of membership. Participants become "members" of a group by mastering a common language, which

also includes unsaid elements, allusions and deictics (etc.), which are not intelligible to non-members.

Enacting collective intelligence

The actions undertaken by members of a group that is part of a collaborative arrangement can thus be viewed as the co-construction of a form of collective intelligence (Levy 1994). This means

> understanding in a more and more precise and operative way how human groups function when they are engaged in a cooperative activity using networked computers or mobile terminals (Levy 2003, 106).

Collective intelligence can take various forms depending on the contexts in which it emerges, the communities and their members. However, its co-construction involves invariable underlying characteristics : local and limited information from each member of the collective, a restricted set of basic rules, multiple and reticular interactions, and an emergent structure that is beneficial to both the individual and the group.

In a general sense, collective intelligence is thus defined as "the emergent behaviour of a heterogeneous network dynamic involving people, technical devices and messages (composed of symbols)" (Levy 2003, 113).

Three types of networks are outlined in a dynamic of interdependence :

— A network of signs (knowledge and messages),
— A network of beings (ethics and people),
— A network of things (abilities and equipment).

The sense of personal efficacy

There is an unbreakable link between an individual and the community in which they evolve. In order for individuals to feel involved in collective evolution, they have to become aware of their relevance and their efficacy within the group. Albert Bandura (1980) developed the concept of the sense of personal efficacy (SPE) and introduced the idea that individuals' subjective perception of their chances of success has a decisive influence on their behaviour.

We employ the concept of SPE to measure its diachronic evolution among the seminar participants.

Analysis of the onscreen enaction of collective intelligence

Here we examine the ethnomethods used by interactants to deal with critical episodes occurring in a polyartefacted, screen-based hybrid experience. How does the group identify and overcome digital bugs and interactional failures in digital interaction and how, simultaneously, does it enact a form of collective intelligence?

Ethological observation of a critical episode

In keeping with our reflexive, ethological and ethnomethodological approach, we start by observing the occurrence of a critical episode (analysis available in the digital version of this manuscript).

Description of a critical episode

We define critical episodes as moments in which communication for one or more participants, who are unwittingly excluded from the participation framework, has to be re-established in real time.

The ex-situ participants could not always easily verbalise a technical problem : verbalisations interrupt the seminar and require the group to focus momentarily on the technology, thus generating an interactional fail. In the case of a conference, for example, giving an alert would mean interrupting the lecturer(s), which could be problematic if the participant(s) were not fully confident in the ability of the group to re-establish communication swiftly.

The lived experience varies for participants situated in different communicative spaces. This asymmetry of perception, along with the impossibility of fully comprehending the subjective experience of the other, leads the participants first to wonder – does the sound problem signalled on Adobe allow adequate listening comfort for the remote participants? Do they need help? Can I do something about the problem or is it simply a bug that I cannot do anything about? Am I capable of intervening? – and then to undertake a collective effort at co-constructing durable ethnomethods that allow them to make communication intelligible and fluid and their activities accountable.

It is also important to make one's own perception intelligible and visible to others, so that they can choose to act (or not) upon obstacles, failures or other bugs.

In the conditions of this experience as it was unfolding, a devolution (Brousseau 1998) was required for the seminar to function smoothly for the remote participants : i.e., responsibility is transferred from the latter who are experiencing difficulties to the participants who are physically present in the seminar room.

On the importance of managing critical episodes and their diachronic evolution.

Disengagement

Critical episodes are thus crucial moments, since how they are dealt with may lead participants to disengage from the situation.

If participants in difficulty did not receive the expected help during the critical episode, this does not mean that the others were indifferent to what they were experiencing. On the contrary, we see that the difficulties of the remote participants also constrained their own participation and made them uncomfortable. At that precise moment (situated at the very start of the seminars), they simply did not know how to deal with the situation and undoubtedly were reluctant to interrupt the guest lecturers yet again.

Diachronic evolution

Our results showed that not only the group's technical skills, but also the sense of personal efficacy (Bandura 1980) of both the group and the individuals over time. The number of technical problems (whether reported or not) did not decrease, but participants became more confident in the group's capacity to resolve them swiftly and efficiently, so that they do not refrain from signalling them when they did occur. This phenomenon is confirmed by the questionnaires completed at the end of each seminar and by the verbal interactions recorded during the seminars, in which we found self-congratulations and references to the fact that the bugs and failures were resolved more and more quickly.

Key points on the subjective experience of participants and recommendations

The focus of our interest here is, more precisely, the first and last questions addressed to the twelve participants in the final assessment questionnaire.

Question 1 : "What are the most striking aspects of your experience in the seminar this year?"

In addressing this question, we can distinguish between approaches depending on the modalities and instantiations of presence. We bring together the responses of members who regularly :

— made use of ex-situ artefacts (Amélie, Christelle, Li-ping, Samira),
— embodied the role of sentinel (Caroline, Jean-François, Joséphine),
— embodied the role of technical or verbal procurator (Christine, Dorothée, Morgane),
— embodied the role of witness (Mabrouka, Yigong)

It should be noted that these categorisations are fluid and dynamic and that a member can be affiliated with several of these categories in practice.

The ex-situ artefacted members have in common the fact that, in their responses, they emphasised their relationship to the artefacts more than to the other participants.

As for the members who regularly embodied the role of sentinel, they point out the permanent need to be alert, as well as the innovative character of the experience, which entailed multidisciplinarity and a divergence of profiles, but a convergence of objectives.

The members who mainly embodied the role of procurator invoke above all the group's benevolence and the solidarity of the collective.

Finally, the members who mainly embodied the role of witness emphasise, above all, the reflexivity and distance taking that is specific to their experience.

The key points identified by the participants in this hybrid experience match the properties of collective intelligence as defined by Pierre Levy (2016). The ex-situ artefacted members highlight the network of things with their focus on resources and equipment; the sentinels, the knowledge network with epistemic and message capital; and the procurators, the network of beings with ethical and social capital. The complementarity of the actors and the maintenance of the networks thus allow this unique group to enact a form of collective intelligence.

Question 4 : "Which advice would you give to someone who would like to use a mixed on-site/remote system?"

Here again, the participants' responses reveal elements that are characteristic of the co-construction of membership and the enaction of collective intelligence transcending interactional failures and digital bugs. The participants who made the recommendations summarised here are indicated in parentheses.

Regarding the network of signs :
— Create shared and participatory online spaces and take notes in them, so that everything is accessible to everyone, anywhere and at any time (Caroline, Christelle).
— Establish rules of communication prior to the hybrid experience (Christine, Jean-François).

Regarding the network of beings :
— Designate specific roles (Christelle, Christine, Samira) or at least choose a moderator to be on the lookout for signs from the participants and to distribute speaking turns (Joséphine) or create in-situ – ex-situ pairs (Samira).
— Develop multimodal attention competencies (Liping, Yigong, Joséphine) and learn how to manage artefactual affordances, gazes and postures (Jean-François).
— Preserve the necessary mutual understanding in the group (Morgane).

Regarding the network of things :
— Integrate the different artefacts gradually within the overall apparatus as each becomes stabilised (Amélie, Dorothée) and choose which to use depending on roles and activities (Christelle, Samira) or make use of a single type of artefact (Mabrouka, Yigong) and, in that case, prioritise the robots (Jean-

François and, more specifically, the Kubi for participants and the Beam for speakers (Christelle).
— Provide back-up equipment and a plan B for all the elements of the apparatus (Caroline) and pay special attention to the quality of the equipment (Morgane) and of the Internet connection (Dorothée).
— Rely on the technical team to install and maintain the digital set-up (Caroline, Christelle, Joséphine, Morgane) or give each participant training in how to use the artefacts or provide a sort of instruction manual for the communication tools (Christine, Jean-François, Samira).

The recommendations make clear that the participants have a common perception of the socio-technical challenges involved and an implicit awareness of the network dynamics underlying the emergence of collective intelligence and based on the complementarity of the members and their confidence in their ability to cooperate. One of the participants formulates the main recommendation that transcends all the others : "accept that technical problems are an integral part of the set-up" (Joséphine). Participants thus simply need "to try to keep the margin of improvisation to a minimum, since something unexpected is going to happen no matter what" (Caroline).

The multidimensional approach in this reflexive ethological study of the enaction of screen presence has elucidated the ecology of the unique experience of a hybrid polyartefacted research seminar in a transdisciplinary way. The ethnomethodological description of a critical episode, along with the transdisciplinary synthesis of the results of the work done along the three main axis of our research and the discursive analysis of the final assessment questionnaires, have revealed what we call the technobodily ethnomethods used by participants to anticipate, work around or resolve incidents that occur during critical episodes.

Our approach to this hybrid experience reveals that identifying and resolving interactional failures and digital bugs requires mutual attention, precautionary face work and distributed agency. Moreover, technical and conversational incidents prove to be beneficial inasmuch as they contribute to the co-construction of collective intelligence (Levy 1994) and enacting a group ethos that does not reduce the number of critical episodes, but qualitatively improves how they are dealt with. This process reinforces the sense of efficacy (Bandura 1980) in both individual and collective capacities for remediation. Presence is maintained in a dynamic process of balance and interdependence among the networks of subjects, of things and of signs.

References

Bandura, Albert. 1980. *L'apprentissage Social*. Bruxelles : P. Mardaga.

Béal, Christine. 2010. *Les Interactions Quotidiennes En Français Et En Anglais : De l'approche Comparative à l'analyse Des Situations Interculturelles*. Bern, Suisse : Peter Lang. Online.

Brousseau, Guy. 1998. *Théorie Des Situations Didactiques : Didactiques Des Mathématiques 1970-1990*. Edited by Nicolas Balacheff, Martin Cooper, and Rosamund Sutherland. Grenoble : La pensée sauvage. Online.

Cosnier, Jacques. 1996. "Les Gestes Du Dialogue : La Communication Non Verbale." *Psychologie de La Motivation* 21 : 129–38. Online.

Garfinkel, Harold. 1967. *Studies in Ethnomethodology*. Reprint. Cambridge, UK : Polity Press. Online.

Kerbrat-Orecchioni, Catherine. 1990. *Les Interactions Verbales. Tome I*. Paris : Armand Colin.

———. 1996. *La Conversation*. Mémo Lettres Sciences Sociales 25. Paris : Éditions du Seuil.

Levy, Pierre. 1994. *L'Intelligence Collective : Pour Une Anthropologie Du Cyberspace*. Paris : Éditions La Découverte.

———. 2003. "Le Jeu de l'intelligence Collective." *Sociétés* 79 (1) : 105–22. Online.

———. 2016. "Cultiver l'intelligence Collective." *Pierre Levy's Blog*. Online.

Mondada, Lorenza. 2006. *La Pertinence Du Contexte Contributions de l'ethnométhodologie Et de l'analyse Conversationnelle*. Verbum, Tome XXVIII. Nancy : Presses universitaires de Nancy. Online.

Quéré, Louis. 1990. "La Pertinence. Communication Et Cognition (Don Sperber Et Deirdre Wilson)." *Réseaux. Communication - Technologie - Société* 8 (42) : 110–11. Online.

Sandré, Marion. 2009. "Analyse d'un Dysfonctionnement Interactionnel – l'interruption – Dans Le Débat de l'entre-Deux-Tours de l'élection Présidentielle de 2007." *Mots. Les Langages Du Politique*, no. 89 (March) : 69–81. Online.

Traverso, Véronique. 1999. *L'analyse Des Conversations*. Collection 128 Linguistique 226. Paris : Nathan.

Vial, Stéphane. 2012. "La Structure de La Révolution Numérique : Philosophie de La Technologie." Thèse de Doctorat en Philosophie de la technologie, Université Paris Descartes. Online.

———. 2013. *L'être Et l'écran : Comment Le Numérique Change La Perception*. Hors Collection. Paris : Presses universitaires de France. Online.

Research training in a polyartefacted doctoral seminar

Morgane Domanchin
Mabrouka El Hachani
Jean-François Grassin

A major question in doctoral training is how to provide support for doctoral students in their appropriation of knowledge that is subject-specific and scientific as well as methodological and technical. As Isabelle Skakni (2011) notes, this training is often experiential, largely informal and unstructured. Doctoral training should be conceived as a process of socialisation to an academic career (Austin 2002), during which doctoral students appropriate a discipline-specific culture that William G. Tierney (1997) defines as a set of symbolic and instrumental activities specific to a given scholarly community. Which stages do doctoral students go through to become acculturated to an academic career and to be socialised? Doctoral seminars are one of the venues in which this process of acculturation and socialisation takes place. These seminars have the advantage of being spread out over a relatively long period of time during a doctoral programme, which reveals a certain progression in the construction of the doctoral student's identity as a researcher.

When the "Digital presence" project was set up within the IMPEC seminar – a project in which the polyartefacted seminar itself was made the object of inquiry – we took the opportunity to study this process of acculturation and research training by way of research. The project entailed new modalities of participation by way of (1) the creation of an instrumented research apparatus and (2) self-reflexive research as part of a visual reflexive ethology approach [44]. We explore how the specific characteristics of the project confi-

---

44. Check "Theoretical and methodological framework for visual reflexive ethology".

guring participation contributed to doctoral students' training.

The aim of this chapter is thus to examine this form of collective work as a space of doctoral training by studying the process of acculturation. By identifying traces of personal engagement in the video data collected during the seminars and the interviews that followed, we investigate how participating in a polyartefacted seminar helps doctoral students develop certain professional and reflexive competencies through their collaboration on a joint research project.

Theoretical and methodological framework

The seminar, in combination with the "Digital Presence" project, was first and foremost a matter of training to do research by doing research, in that the doctoral students were expected to participate in all the stages of the project. The students' participatory thinking, modes of behaviour and actions come together in these stages, developing their socio-technical and scientific competencies. The project was launched and piloted by Christine and was configured for her doctoral seminar, for both training and research.

The seminar was designed to enable doctoral students to develop academic, technical and methodological competencies in collaborative situations that facilitated individual engagement and provided a supportive environment.

The seminar as a venue for developing specific competencies

In research training, Philippe Perrenoud (1995) underscores the importance of acquiring theoretical and disciplinary knowledge as well as "competencies related to the scholarly profession in a given discipline and in the corresponding organisations" (1995, 23). We explore the processes that help students need to acquire the competencies related to the academic profession which Perrenoud refers to. Few studies have been conducted thus far on the competencies acquired in doctoral training programmes, even if competency dictionaries are currently being implemented in Switzerland and Quebec.

Three additional competencies can be added that correspond to our specific research situation : communicative competencies, collaborative competencies and semiotechnical competencies related to the artefactual set-up. Setting up a research project focusing on the seminar itself as its object, with a special interest in its polyartefactual dimension, involved participants de facto in a project of co-construction. This provided them with a co-responsibility that was elaborated and carried out from one seminar session to the next through the constitution of a corpus and the construction of a research object. This very demanding form of personal engagement promoted the development of an academic ethos, and we examine how these competencies arose in self-reflexive discourse and over the course of the collaborative work sessions in the seminar.

The polyartefacted seminar as a collaborative situation

The learning situation that we are examining is in fact a highly collaborative situation. The definition of the word "seminar" in the French online dictionary Trésor de la Langue Française informatisé (TLFi) emphasises the collective and collaborative nature of this time devoted to discussion and exchange on a subject related to professional activity. For Wendy L. Bedwell et al. (2012), collaboration is "an evolving process whereby two or more social entities actively and reciprocally engage in joint activities aimed at achieving at least one shared goal" (Bedwell et al. 2012, 130).

As Mabrouka El Hachani explains, collaboration is the intertwining of these processes and entails "engaging in a joint action (cooperation), discussing this joint action (communication), and basing work on the organisation of interdependent tasks and actions that need to be carried out (coordination) to achieve the goal that has been set" (El Hachani 2014, 228). In this seminar, communication and coordination resources are highly polyartefacted. The doctoral training support organisation (Conférence Permanente des Directeurs.trices de laboratoires en Sciences de l'Information et de la Communication, CPDirSIC) notes that :

> By being involved in the life of the research group, doctoral students acquire precise and up-to-date theoretical and methodological knowledge. Research units also provide a context within which doctoral students experience socialisation to academic professions, as well as other professions requiring a high level of expertise, such as when they are involved in contracts.

The seminar and the ethos of the young researcher

The collaborative situation of the seminar provided the opportunity to study the role occupied by the team's doctoral students and the ethos they were constructing.

But which kind of academic ethos are we talking about? As Emmanuelle Leclercq and Danielle Potocki Malicet (2006, 1) note :

> From the point of view of academic actors, there is not one academic profession, but many, which are largely structured by socio-professional membership, and a plurality of professional identities.

The array of academic profiles is quite rich, and it shows the degree to which the researcher is associated with a discipline or a research network or even a form of independence that is a described as a "professional career". The authors point to an important distinction between academic profession and academic identity. If the former is common to all, the latter, on the contrary, leads to notable differences in the construction of professional identity as well as related work values. The question follows as to which models form the basis of the construction of the young researcher's ethos.

In this chapter, we study how the identities of young researchers are constructed within a situation of polyartefactual collaboration by the student's use of certain competencies. Our study analyses the competencies perceived and utilised by doctoral students in collaborative activities during the research project. Through our study of the discursive and pragmatic process of this construction in the action of the seminar, we present the concept of identity posture of legitimacy.

Methodology

In light of the fact that doctoral work is a poorly documented field as such, we adopt an ecological perspective to show its complexity. The four people conducting doctoral studies in the research team were not at the same stage of their thesis when the data was collected and the seminar was held. We hypothesised that this would have an impact on the expression of their academic ethos.

A cross-analysis of the reflexive interviews of the four doctoral students participating in the seminar and of the video recordings of the different sessions lead us to two types of analyses. We conducted both a content analysis examining epistemic postures, i.e., with respect to knowledge and competencies, and a discourse analysis of discursive enunciation and the construction of a discursive ethos (Maingueneau 2014) that distinguishes between "declared ethos (what speakers say about themselves) and observed ethos (what their manner of enunciation shows)" (2014, 34). The analysis of enunciative postures during the interviews reveals the construction of identity postures of legitimacy based on the collaborative situation and the individual's identity as a young researcher.

Case study

The polyartefacted seminar as a conducive environments to doctoral training

We will now describe three general characteristics of the seminar that were conducive to doctoral training; then we will paint four individual portraits to show how students' participation lead to their engagement in the project.

An extended space and time for doctoral training

In comparison to the space and time constraints of a traditional doctoral seminar, the polyartefacted seminar has a more extended range. The doctoral seminar and the "Digital Presence" research project were marked by four different stages in time.

1. In the initial stage, setting up the seminar in technical terms presupposed a logistical installation involving the preparation of the telepresence artefacts and the material for collecting data.

2. The technical artefacts had to be set up for each session of the seminar to be able to take place. Once the artefacts were connected, in-situ and ex-situ participants were responsible for opening the proceedings when they arrived and also for bringing them to a close.

3. The data collected was then digitised and posted online : first in a private space shared by the mem-

bers of the research team, and then, once the data was organised, on the Ortolang platform.

4. These two spaces allowed participants to consult the data.

Complexified collaboration

As we have just seen, collaboration in the seminar was based on a complex apparatus.

The multiplicity of the spaces produced is a source of complexity and sometimes requires multple activities. But it can also be the source of more varied participation frameworks than in a traditional configuration, thus encouraging different forms of involvement that help develop the ethos of the young researchers.

Shared expertise

The polyartefactual dimension of the seminar imposed a novel dimension on all the participants, which appeared to be conducive to the inclusion of the doctoral students. For instance, as a researcher and the seminar coordinator, Christine's expertise was acknowledged, but her status as "conductor" and her role in hosting guest speakers left the task of dealing with the research apparatus during the sessions to some of the participants. Over the course of the seminar, the technical competencies of the participants and, in particular, of the doctoral students were called upon in order to ensure that the technical set-up was working properly. As this set-up was complex and new to all the members, they shared responsibility for keeping it in good working order, and its highly technical dimension required complimentary forms of expertise. Depending on scientific or technical knowledge and competencies, participatory regimes were able to emerge which placed certain participants at the interface between different areas of expertise.

We will now illustrate the development of these competencies and analyse the postures of the four doctoral students in the seminar.

Identities of the junior researchers

Yigong

The traces of scientific and technical development that can be observed in the interviews conducted with the doctoral students vary depending on the situation of the doctoral student during the seminar as an in-situ or ex-situ participant. Yigong, a first-year in-situ doctoral student, described the seminar in his interview as a "new scientific experience".

Although the topics covered were not directly connected to his thesis [45], Yigong says that he discovered "some concepts, but not a lot". These discoveries led him to carry out internet searches while the seminar was going on, which sometime limited his participation in favour of note-taking.

In the reflexive interview, this choice leads him to wonder about the nature of his participation in the seminar or rather of the other group members' perception of him, in order to affirm his belonging :

> For me I don't feel like I'm absent, but I think, since I still don't speak very well, I think for other people I am kind of absent from the seminar.

Yigong explains what he means by "being present" and hence the actual actions that this participation entails :

> Being present means... I feel, because I'm focused on taking notes and thinking about what is being said and sometimes on finding bibliographies, so I feel very

---

45. Yigong is writing a thesis on digital literacy in the Chinese educational context.

present. Though I think compared to the others, I'm maybe kind of absent.

A first posture that can be identified in the interviews, and that we call an institutional legitimacy posture, is situated along a present/not-present axis. This posture is summarised by one's own and others' perception of one's legitimacy in the group. Being present is being able to defend this legitimacy. In Yigong's case, presence is so problematic that his concerns about this legitimacy are thematised in his reflexive interview. In the case of the three other doctoral students whose interviews will be analysed in the following sections, this takes place via the assertion of socio-technical competencies, which allow the student either to make herself present to others (Amélie) or to make all the members of the group present (Dorothée), or by a role identity as an interface between the groups (Morgane).

Amélie

Amélie's posture within the seminar is constructed in a completely different way for two fundamental reasons : as a third-year doctoral student, Amélie is already working on telepresence robots and will participate in all the sessions using the Beam device. She thus forges an identity in the group via an artefactual presence and her developing expertise.

The importance that Amélie attaches to resolving technical problems – to making communication more fluid in the group's interaction by using technical competencies related to the manipulation of the robot and the software interfaces – can be explained by her desire to be involved in the research project. An inclusive "*on*" – in the sense of "we" rather than "they" – appears in her discourse and expresses her being part of the group of researchers ("for me it's important actually to say that it's properly framed be-

cause it's important that we [*on*] have good data after all",
"what we [*on*] are doing has a certain scientific level after
all"). This discourse shows both the participant's difficulty
and her desire to be fully involved in the situation, despite
the distance and the (over)exposure entailed by her presence via the robot. The robot allowed her to be present
but at the same time it also isolated and exposed her. The
telepresence apparatus gave Amélie the means to be involved, but also entailed two correlated risks : isolation from
the group and overexposure with respect to the position
that she would like to have in it. For Amélie, the solution
lay in the intensity of her engagement. She became involved in phases 2 and 4 of the project : the phase of holding
the seminar, of course, but also the data visualisation phase
– a retrospective activity that uses the research apparatus to
increase competence by way of reflexivity.

Dorothée

The figure of Dorothée is in some ways similar to that of
Amélie. Dorothée was also in her third year of doctoral studies during the seminar. She is a specialist in telepresence
robots : her research deals with their educational uses. However, Dorothée was attended the seminar in-situ in her
case.

One of the strategies employed by Dorothée to participate
in the seminar was to assign herself a role in managing the
technical telepresence apparatus.

An anecdote that she tells in the interview is revealing of
the importance that she attaches to the construction of the
scientific research and the role that she claims for herself.
She explains that she was not physically present during one
seminar and that the Adobe Connect system did not make
it technically possible for her to intervene and defend her
research personally.

Dorothée claims a researcher's identity related to her expertise, but, on this occasion, she does not manage to have it
confirmed for technical reasons related to intervening remotely. The identity posture is thematised in her discourse
along a "competent/incompetent" axis in scientific matters.
But during this episode, the apparatus fails to make the
participants equally present in the seminar. The apparatus
thus interrupts the collaboration and isolates the young researcher, who finds this all the more difficult inasmuch she
makes a very strong claim to her place in the peer group.

Morgane

Our last portrait is that of Morgane. Morgane plays a key
role in the seminar, since she is involved in all four phases
(preparation, holding the seminar, digitisation, and consul-
tation of the data). In the "Digital Presence" project, she
held the status of research assistant to Christine, who was
her doctoral supervisor. This status gave her several respon-
sibilities de facto. We will analyse the process of acquisition
of competencies and her posture in three phases : (1) by
examining her role as interface between the research team
and the technical team responsible for collecting the data ;
(2) by examining her note-taking ; and (3) by studying her
legitimacy posture.
Morgane's role of interface [46] between two teams involved
taking into account the research objects during the phase
of setting up the apparatus.
Morgane had a very strong sense of the spatiotemporal extension of the seminar.
In her discourse, Morgane uses the French pronoun *on* in an
extremely wide variety of ways. This proliferation of *on* and

---

46. In the interview, Morgane explains this role : "As for me, my
function is really, so to speak, to be responsible for setting up the
LiPen apparatus and also to be the technical support."

of its references in her discourse reveals a participant who is constructing her identity in belonging to various groups corresponding to different roles that she takes on during the research process.

Morgane experiences the research project as a flow, she no longer distinguishes the technical discussions that take place outside the seminar, but that are an integral part of the research project. These discussions also illustrate the process of team building and of cooperation. The work team instantiates a form of collaboration involving individuals, and cooperation refers to individual orientation in a work team. Morgane is at the centre of this system of exchange between the Cellule Corpus Complexes (CCC)[47] and the research team that allowed the work team to be constructed. She cooperated with the CCC team for the purpose of the collaborative process.

Intertwining digital spaces thus promotes both the production of scientific knowledge, by supporting collaboration, and research training, by varying the possibilities of participation.

Whereas the other doctoral students thematise their position in the seminar along a "present/not present" or "legitimate/not legitimate" axis, Morgane adopts a posture of legitimacy that is marked on the side of cooperation.

We can note the appearance in her discourse of an "idealised" figure of the researcher who is able to participate in the scientific discussion, to make her voice and her knowledge heard whereas this is a figure that minimises the technical and material aspect of research for which the junior researcher is responsible. Now, the competency claimed by Morgane is this ability "to be able to propose solutions quickly, also to be able to judge the solutions proposed by others".

---

47. Complex Corpora Center.

We are thus able to observe via these illustrations how the format of the polyartefacted seminar invites participants to appropriate a variety of research, technical, scientific and collaborative competencies. When put into practice, they are always situated adaptive competencies.

Discussion

The seminar genre [48] and its expectations undergo renewal in a professional field both by virtue of its polyartefactual dimension, allowing for remote presence and creating spaces for complex participation frameworks, and by virtue of the support of a reflexive research project that promotes the development of socio-technical and scientific competencies and a rich disciplinary socialisation.

A supported training situation

During the the seminar, the doctoral students were given the opportunity to speak freely, in order to facilitate their integration into the group.

As we have seen, this strong aspect of speaking up is imposed upon the doctoral students who have understood this fact and who are constructing their posture vis-à-vis this opportunity to be seized. The technical dimension on which the polyartefacted seminar is based is then added to this. This dimension requires specific competencies that some senior researchers do not always possess. The complementarity of competencies thus becomes essential for the smooth functioning of the seminar.

Taking into account the heterogeneity of the professional statuses of the participants, which is a classic element in the ecology of a doctoral seminar, is thus highlighted. But,

---

48. In Yves Clot's sense : "a sedimentation and prolongation of prior joint activities… which has been done by previous generations of a given milieu" (1999, 37).

above all, this calls into question the importance of a strictly scientific expertise for the purpose of training. Collaboration is constructed by way of the attribution of certain well-defined roles prior to the sessions, and these roles are supported by processes of cooperation over the course of the seminar.

The use of the French pronoun *on* in the reflexive discourse of the participants highlights how the speakers studied position themselves vis-à-vis a figure of the research group.

These enunciative postures regarding the construction of a collective instantiation that is diversely expressed by *on* in the different forms of discourse thus have their complement in an analysis of "I" and the conditions of emergence of subjects by way of the enunciative affirmation of role identities or postures of legitimacy. We have identified three postures of legitimacy throughout our case study that make the doctoral student legitimate in the situation and that students develop via the utilisation of competencies :

1. a posture based on the legitimacy of presence, which we call on-site legitimacy posture;
2. a posture based on scientific legitimacy, which we call epistemic legitimacy posture;
3. a posture based on the legitimacy of the relationship to the other, which demands reliability and which we call pragmatic legitimacy posture.

By analysing discourse and action, we saw how these postures could be combined in a posture of multiple legitimacy, thus contributing to the doctoral student's training.

Conclusion

The doctoral seminar is the venue of the social process of construction of identity via the acquisition of certain roles and certain particular competencies, and this is all the more the case in a polyartefacted seminar. The specificity of poly-artefactual seminar is that it is based on a relatively strong technical dimension, both in terms of remote communication and modalities of collaboration. In this configuration, the acquisition of technical competencies plays a key role in getting participants involved in the group, in particular, for doctoral students who are at an advanced stage in their training and who have a research topic closely related to the theme of the seminar project. The polyartefacted seminar promotes learning by doing and acting in real time and within a collaborative process. It also provides a reflexive, interdisciplinary space that promotes disciplinary openness for the doctoral students by multiplying the zones of proximal development.

This chapter examined the elaboration of a space of scientific discussion that is fundamental for research training. We have highlighted several salient points about the co-construction of this collaborative space and the processes it entails. Traces of the co-construction of group cooperation and the construction of work routines were emphasised and present evidence of a supported elaboration of research skills. Our study suggests that participation in a research project allows cultures and identities to develop that are key for research training (Sinclair, Barnacle, and Cuthbert 2014). The seminar is in fact "a performance, a practice, something that not only happens, in time and space, a choreography of bodies and voices, but is repeated, rehearsed and cited" (Green 2009, 248). This choreography allows doctoral students to observe and learn, and to develop competencies that are specific to the community they belong to. It is also a challenge in which the young researcher is anything but ontologically secure and which entails the creation of emotionally safe environments that the members maintain through the artefacted set-up and in being attentive to others[49]. The discursive ethos analysed here shows traces of this learning process and identity construction of the young researchers. Finally, the particularity of this type of research project, in which the participants take part in exercises of self-analysis (in the first and second person[50]), trains them for a subjectifying activity that is especially conducive to the construction of a critical and normative ethos.

Our study confirms the importance of others and self-validations in the construction of one's identity as a researcher (Mantai 2015). These role identities in collaborative research are emphasised in different ways by the doctoral students, even if there are certain recurrent roles : the epistemic value of professional identity was found in the discourse of all the participants, some of them insisting on the problematic legitimacy that this identity entails for them. The identity as a researcher requires a participatory presence and a legitimacy for which they will need validation from other members of the group. For some, moreover, collaborative work in a polyartefacted situation seems to impose an identity that is validated in terms of reliability.

Finally, we showed the triple process-oriented heuristic aspect that is present in the situation : a doctoral seminar that is (1) scholarly, (2) highly artefactual, and (3) supported by a research project. This heuristic process interweaves the construction of ethos, apparatus and knowledge. Scientific and technical competencies are constructed along with the development of identity postures of legitimacy.

---

49. Check "Attentional affordances in an instrumented seminar".

50. Check "Theoretical and methodological framework for visual reflexive ethology".

References

Austin, Ann E. 2002. "Preparing the Next Generation of Faculty : Graduate School as Socialization to the Academic Career." *The Journal of Higher Education* 73 (1) : 94–122. Online.

Bedwell, Wendy L., Jessica L. Wildman, Deborah Diaz-Granados, Maritza Salazar, William S. Kramer, and Eduardo Salas. 2012. "Collaboration at Work : An Integrative Multilevel Conceptualization." *Human Resource Management Review*, Construct Clarity in Human Resource Management Research, 22 (2) : 128–45. Online.

Clot, Yves. 1999. *La Fonction Psychologique Du Travail*. 1ère édition. Le Travail Humain. Paris : Presses universitaires de France.

El Hachani, Mabrouka. 2014. "Les Dispositifs Collaboratifs En Contexte Professionnel : Mutualisation Et Unités Documentaires, Entre Dynamique Collective Et Réflexion Individuelle." In *Didactiques Et Métiers de l'humain Et de La Relation : Nouveaux Espaces Et Dispositifs En Question, Nouveaux Horizons En Formation Et En Recherche : Objets de Recherche Et Pratiques "En Écloserie"*, edited by Muriel Frisch. Paris : L'Harmattan. Online.

Green, Bill. 2009. "Framing Doctoral Education as Practice." In *Changing Practices of Doctoral Education*, edited by David Boud and Alison Lee, 239–48. London ; New York : Routledge. Online.

Leclercq, Emmanuelle, and Danielle Potocki Malicet. 2006. "Identités Professionnelles Et Métiers Des Chercheurs." In *XVIIe Congrès de l'association Francophone de Gestion Des Ressources Humaines*, 12. Reims. Online.

Maingueneau, Dominique. 2014. "Retour Critique Sur l'éthos." *Langage Et Société* 149 (3) : 31–48. Online.

Mantai, Lilia. 2015. "Feeling Like a Researcher : Experiences of Early Doctoral Students in Australia." *Studies in Higher Education*, 1–15. Online.

Perrenoud, Philippe. 1995. "Des Savoirs Aux Compétences, de Quoi Parle-t-on En Parlant de Compétences ?" In, 9 :20–24. Association québécoise de pédagogie collégiale. Online.

Sinclair, Jennifer, Robyn Barnacle, and Denise Cuthbert. 2014. "How the Doctorate Contributes to the Formation of Active Researchers : What the Research Tells Us." *Studies in Higher Education* 39 (10) : 1972–86. Online.

Skakni, Isabelle. 2011. "Socialisation Disciplinaire Et Persévérance Aux Études Doctorales : Une Analyse Des Sphères Critiques." *Initio* 1 : 18–34. Online.

Tierney, William G. 1997. "Organizational Socialization in Higher Education." *The Journal of Higher Education* 68 (1) : 1–16. Online.

Conclusion

Christine Develotte

This volume is the first publication of the results of the collective research that we carried out between 2016 and 2020.

This concluding chapter aims to look at the conceptual aspects of our work and at its collective, reflexive and open experiential form.

The research we have carried out has without doubt a militant aspect. This research is, in itself, an epistemological manifesto establishing, in this particular techno-historical moment, the interdisciplinarity and hybridity of methodologies as unavoidable, the force of the group as key in the research process bringing together different disciplines and (technological) cultures, and open science via the intermediary of a digital form of publication as the preferred mode to publicise scientific results.

Starting from the two initial objectives of this volume, we describe how we proceeded and how other perspectives emerged along the way.

The study of interaction in a polyartefacted situation

From a scientific point of view, the first research objective, formulated once the data collection was finished, was the following :

> To study empirically what telepresence does to a doctoral seminar, the impact it has on the participants and on the dynamics of the exchanges that take place (Develotte 2018, 171).

This very broad formulation sought to give free rein to the researchers to determine which aspects they regarded as relevant to study. Moreover, the data collection set-up was designed according to scientific perspectives rooted in different approaches; this multidisciplinarity lead us to give priority to a data collection protocol employing a qualitative procedure in keeping with current practice in humanities and social sciences.

Theoretical and methodological alliances came into being during the analyses in light of the complexity of the apparatus that had been established and the multimodality of the data collected. Thus, the study of corporeality combined phenomenology and psychology in an analysis at the crossroads of visual ethnography, the multimodal analysis of interaction and phenomenological analysis; the analyses of attention merged phenomenology and communication sciences in a multimodal analysis; the analysis of habituation (bugs and failures) undertook an ethnomethodological analysis and drew on phenomenology, psychology and anthropology (collective intelligence). In an ethnological, multimodal approach, the study of politeness combined Goffmanian microsociology, discourse analysis and evolutionary biology.

This disciplinary heterogeneity is apparent in the general bibliography : among the 112 authors cited in the different chapters, fewer than 20% are associated with linguistics, 21% work in the fields of sociology and anthropology, 20% in psychology and communication, 27% in philosophy and education, and around 12% belong to other disciplines (design, human-machine interaction, biology, marketing or even dance).

To grasp the interactional specificities generated in the context of the complex-situation studied here, we thus gave priority to conceptual and methodological hybrids from the humanities and social sciences.

The analyses that we carried out on the different aspects of the seminar on this basis have allowed us to theorise the different stages of mediation (immediation, demediation, remediation) and the roles played by the participants who were in turn sentinels, procurators and witnesses[51]. With respect to interactional specificities, we explored the opposition between artefactual and personal terms of address and proposed conversational maxims[52]. Involuntary or appropriated artefactual presence was studied in terms of over-ratification, hyper-exposure or hypo-exposure[53]. Looking at attentional choreographies revealed the emergence of attentional co-affordances in this polyartefacted context[54].

Towards open science

The second objective consisted of inscribing our research in open science : we chose digital publishing as a solution that would make our data openly available to the research community. This volume, which represents the first stage in our data analysis, concentrates on the most surprising or remarkable phenomena and thus only exploits a very small amount of the data we gathered. Opening the corpus up to the research community may give others an opportunity to study the data in dimensions different from ours and that will nourish our approach.

The need for digital publication became apparent during the project when it became clear that a print edition could only provide a highly reductive account of the analyses. As a consequence, the members of the research group were faced with the need to develop new competencies, going beyond the simple selection of relevant excerpts and the creation of a video capsule, in order to move towards an

---

51. Check "Artefacted intercorporeality, between reification and personification".

52. Check "New norms of politeness in digital contexts".

53. Check "Autonomy and artefactual presence in a polyartefacted seminar".

54. Check "Attentional affordances in an instrumented seminar".

annotation of these capsules in a format compatible with digital publishing. The need for new professions became apparent in order to supplement the work of the research team with IT, documentary and technical expertise. Our team of researchers from the humanities and social sciences were themselves led to enrich their palette with new competencies, some of them derived from the group, which thus again shows its added value.

New perspectives for future research on the multimodality of the data have thus been opened up. Digital publication constitutes a new challenge for the definition of a format for analysing screen interactions that can take into account the complexity of these multimodal interactions entailing different spaces (in Lyon and elsewhere). This format involves both the researcher's own perspective on the data and what they would like to show readers via the norms of digital publishing.

Beyond these two objectives, the experiential form of this research that is simultaneously collective, reflexive and open turned out to be key and deserves to be explicitly discussed.

A collective reflexive experience

The collective dimension of the project played a fundamental role in the scientific experiment that was conducted. The reflexive approach was adopted by the group, and because the participants trusted one another, they agreed to cooperate in an undertaking aiming at developing collective intelligence starting from individual competencies. Everyone was invited to contribute research to several chapters, thus forging a comprehensive view of the whole. Review and revision of the first drafts was undertaken as a group, so as to bring together all the complexity of the points of view around the aspect being studied. The project thus channelled the participants' energies toward a common goal whose result is of greater value for the group than for the individual researcher.

In what follows, we will examine this reflexive dimension that constitutes the specificity of this work and its implications both for our research and the different participants.

Reflexive ethology led us to work on and with people all sharing the same situation and the same ambition of analysing behaviour. The research posture of each of the people participating in the interviews led them to formulate extensive and detailed responses to the interviewer's questions and provided material for analysis; everyone kept in mind that their own responses would not only serve to supplement their own collection of data and hence their own analyses, but also those of the group as a whole. By sharing feelings and common experience, the group consolidated our socio-affective ties, as if we together went through the same ordeal: the research process more than the seminar as such!

Our chosen scientific approach led the members of the research team to work on videos in which they themselves appear, giving rise to an effect of a "first-person science success story". Therefore, the strategy we adopted in the chapters of this volume was more one of avoidance, in the sense that the researchers did not analyse their own words or behaviour, but rather those of their colleagues (who were actually sometimes collaborating with them on the same chapter). The members of the research team were thus confronted with the peculiar situation of being written about by their colleagues, producing disturbing, intrusive effects. This oddity is based, in particular, on the temptation to give one's own interpretation of the excerpt and on the expropriation, as researchers, of an analysis that they could imagine carrying out themselves [55].

We can pause for a moment to reflect on the specific difficulties created by the analysis by the group of the very group to which each participant belongs.

As a consequence of the efforts made in the analyses to de-subjectivise observed forms of behaviour, the participants are dehumanised, or reified. This gives rise to a particular type of frustration for the researchers-participants being studied, who, when reading the chapters, are put in a position of having to accept seeing their behaviour "reduced" only to the analytical criteria adopted. As Pierre Bourdieu notes :

> the concern to keep the analysis as close to "concrete reality" as possible ... can prompt us entirely to miss a "reality" that escapes immediate intuition because it resides in structures that are transcendent to the interaction they inform (1992, 119–20).

The researchers faced with a novel experience :to come to terms with everything that was left unsaid when one particular aspect was highlighted, which did not, for example, take into account the history of interpersonal relations and their intertext.

One of the surprises during the analyses – i.e., after the recording of the videos – was realising how difficult it was to "take the other's place", when coming to grasp the different constraints or when it became clear retrospectively how poorly one or the other participant was seeing or hearing and the extent to which we may ourselves have lacked empathy at the very beginning of the seminar. One of the participants had not understood that her image could be seen and consequently had not prepared herself physically

---

55. Even if one can agree that the analysis contributes an interpretation that is complementary to the first-person interpretation by taking into account realities that escaped the person observed.

(getting dressed, putting on make-up, doing her hair). As she was filmed where she lived, she felt "at home", and she found it to be repeated torture to see her image projected on the screen in a light that was not compatible with the image she adopts publicly. We see from this example that during this first phase of data collection in the seminar, this participant viewed herself as, above all, a "researcher participating in a seminar" and not yet as a "researcher producing a reflexive ethological analysis", having not yet taken up this second posture as an analyst.

Thus, if the members of the research team "gave their bodies to science" in a sense, they also let go by trusting their peers to analyse the interaction for them. This is all the more the case since the analyses often point out malfunctions and situations in which the participant-researcher is not necessarily seen in a flattering way. From this perspective, we decided to open up access to the corpus under certain conditions, such as not using family names (first names were not changed, however, since this seemed too artificial to us). The publication on the Ateliers de [sens public] platform, combined with the Hypothes.is annotation tool, accentuates these aspects, since the volume will be open to commentary by the scientific community as a whole on this platform.

In effect, as a result of opening up access to the data and the published analyses, our self-images are exposed outside of the group : i.e., in contrast to the rather confidential form of communication specific to the seminar, which is traditionally a closed space that is inaccessible to a non-participant. The rules of conversation in the seminar followed a pre-established format, but they were also co-constructed and forged by habit. Not everything was necessarily of the order of the "showable"; but here we accepted to show what went on "backstage" : the members of the research team involved in the very construction of the research and the elaboration of protocols, technical and theoretical apparatuses, thus revealing all the modes of behaviour and forms of interaction that occur prior to producing the finished product, whether an article or book.

The endangering of the self in this undertaking comes from the fact that we chose to collect the data while the group was learning to use new communication tools. This phase of appropriation necessarily involved going astray : failures that disturbed the "normal" progress of the seminar, beyond the usual trial and error that is inherent to any research process. Moreover, all the participants did not have the same level of technical expertise related to the artefacts, and these differences between the members modified the usual hierarchy associated solely with scientific knowledge. If digital publishing thus opens up new horizons that allow us to conceive of the possibility of sharing complex data with the research community in the form of open science, the question of the degree of openness that we are able to tolerate at the end of the experience remains unanswered. In an era of self-exposure, how far is it possible for a researcher to go ? This exploration of limits becomes an integral part of the research process in the context of a movement towards open science formats, involving boundaries to be stipulated within protocols for sharing and anonymisation of data that have still to be invented, while taking into account possible forms of abuse.

The entirety of the process allowed us to experience both positions : on the one hand, the difficulty involved in making someone visible who has not asked for it (for example, the speakers) and, on the other, one's own experience of being placed under observation for scholarly purposes.

The seminar as a heuristic situation

If we look at the educational dimension of this collective research project, the form of the seminar may itself have been heuristic. In fact, the "nurturing matrix" (Kern and Develotte 2018) put into place, including technological and human dimensions, contained a zone of proximal development in itself, both on the scholarly and on the technical level [56]. This matrix was nourished, moreover, by the regularity of the sessions and the attention that each of the participants gave to the work of the others, thus putting the socio-affective dimensions of interpersonal relationships at the very heart of the research set-up.

In this context, a sense of efficacy (Bandura 2003) thus came into being that was no longer personal, but rather distributed, collective, systemic and processual [57], and that would be interesting to study in greater detail.

From the point of view of doctoral training, the project contributed to a new way of understanding the doctoral supervisor as a witness, as coined by Bacon and Midgelow (2019) in the context of the "Artistic Doctorates in Europe" project (ADIE 2016-2019). The doctoral training programme recounted by the authors is based, like our experience, on collective work and the Peer-to-Peer Feedback Chain, as well as on the creative process whose point of departure is the self and its auto-ethnography : "Finding ways in which practitioner/scholars (including mySelf) can 'articulate something' and from the creative process using the Self as source for creativity or auto/Self-ethnography" (Bacon and Midgelow 2019). Research is seen as a creative, co-relational, collective and networked process :

---

56. Check "Research training in a polyartefacted doctoral seminar".

57. Check "Digital bugs and interactional fails in the service of collective intelligence".

> We illuminate, and hopefully inspire, ways of going about and supporting research as a creative, co-relational, collective and networked process » (Bacon and Midgelow 2019, 3, preface).

In this collective creative context, the experience of "practice as research" in all the stages of the research project is offered to the different participants, and in the understanding that the humanities and social sciences will also be able to benefit from these new postures in doctoral training programmes.

Finally, now that the team adventure has been completed, what are the "shared memories [58]" of the participants? Although no data was collected among the different members in the aftermath of the project, we can imagine that shared memory will be experienced differently depending on the degree of engagement, the attendance of each participant and the interest taken during these four years of joint work. Nonetheless, it seems that at least one aspect is common to all : namely, the element of unpredictability involved in every stage, which gave the research, which was conducted over a short period, the aspect of an "adventure". Testing out the equipment as an integral part of the data collected or choosing to publish in a digital format, without having grasped everything that this entailed at the time of the decision, aroused curiosity that was often mixed with uncertainty, but that always stimulated the participants to confront the next stages.

---

58. For Louise Merzeau, "the notion of sharing allows us to grasp crucial aspects of the very dynamic of the commons by emphasising processes rather than things" (2017, 171).

In the footsteps of prior research

Finally, if we take another look at the studies that provided inspiration for this research, we find many aspects that resonate with our experience.

The project in which Gregory Bateson participated starting in 1955 (McQuown 1971) experimented with new recording equipment (the video camera) that inspired a new perspective on interaction. In 2016, we also called upon technical innovations; a 360° camera and a remote-controlled webcam. Just like us, Bateson was quite uncomfortable seeing his postural-facial-gestural behaviour dissected on screen by his colleagues : "there were for me moments of considerable pain when the others were interpreting my actions, and I was forced to see those actions on the screen" (Bateson 1958, 99). As we saw previously, even if seeing oneself is still a sensitive matter, we can argue that times have changed, given the contemporary social environment of selfies and reality television, the relationship to self-image is nowadays experienced differently.

In their conclusion to *Décrire la conversation*, Cosnier et al. noted that in their volume they had overcome "linguists' aversion to using tape recorders or video recorders" (1987, 358). The situation has changed significantly in 30 years, even if the researchers at that time seem to have shared the same emotions related to long-term innovative work in their group : "During the long hours of work on this corpus, we went a thousand times from irritation to amusement, from discouragement to excited attention" (1987, 358). Nonetheless, they ended on a very positive note :

> By virtue of its paltry banality, the corpus appeared to us to be representative precisely of ordinary conversation : it reveals basic and very general rules of the social game of encounter ….By way of the convergence of heterogeneous clues, it allowed us to discover the

importance of interactional regulation, to define the proper object of joint research (total interaction) and a point of view well adapted to this object (multidisciplinarity).

Their last sentence appears as if addressed to us :

These convictions are recent… in large part, they thus have still to be put into practice (1987, 359).

This same interdisciplinary desire inspired the 2011 project *Décrire la conversation en ligne* ("Describing online conversation"). In the conclusion and, more precisely, in the section "Perspectives on the future of research in this field", the authors observed :

We can thus consider the research field to be ready to tackle these new types of data. These emerging forms of complementarity that appear between the methodological contributions on conversation, on environment and spaces. Our volume has outlined these forms; they remain to be confirmed and materialised within international and interdisciplinary collaborations (Develotte, Kern, and Lamy 2011, 200).

The volume also discussed opening up access to the corpus on an international level and to the research community :

The globalised corpora of communication that researchers will be sure to gather in a future characterised by the lightning-quick dissemination of the tools will need these cross-cultural perspectives (Develotte, Kern, and Lamy 2011, 200).

As for the publishing format outlined :

These changes will have an effect on the form in which research will be presented – the presentation will be more and more multimodal and hence difficult to publish on paper. Markee and Stansell (2007), for example, maintain that the integration of information in the form of video, audio, text and image is no longer a luxury and that, on the contrary, it has become a necessity for establishing more rigorous standards of research : above all, for elements that are difficult to transcribe, such as gestures, facial expressions, gazes, and postures (Develotte, Kern, and Lamy 2011, 201).

This is precisely the direction in which the continuation of our research in the humanities and the social sciences is heading, since we have chosen a digital format that we are working on in different respects (annotated video resources, hypertext links, metadata). In keeping with the experience of this research that led us to "open a path by walking [59]" (Machado 1917), we thus conclude this version of our work barely knowing in what form it will be published.

References

Bacon, Jane, and Vida Midgelow. 2019. "Reconsidering Research and Supervision as Creative Embodied Practice." *ADiE*. Online.

Bandura, Albert. 2003. *Auto-Efficacité : Le Sentiment d'efficacité Personnelle*. Translated by Jacques Lecomte. Première édition. Ouvertures Psychologiques. Paris : De Boeck Université.

Bateson, Gregory. 1958. "Language and Psychotherapy, Frieda Fromm-Reichmann's Last Project." *Psychiatry* 21 (1) : 96–100.

Bourdieu, Pierre. 1992. *Réponses : Pour Une Anthropologie Réflexive*. Edited by Loïc Wacquant. Libre Examen. Paris : Éditions du Seuil.

---

59. "*se hace camino al anda*" (Machado 1917).

Cosnier, Jacques, Catherine Kerbrat-Orecchioni, and Robert Bouchard. 1987. *Décrire La Conversation*. Lyon : Presses universitaires de Lyon. Online.

Develotte, Christine. 2018. "Un Dispositif d'études de La Téléprésence Dans Un Séminaire Doctoral : L'atelier Exploratoire Présences Numériques." In *La Téléprésence En Formation*, edited by Jean-Luc Rinaudo, 171–93. ISTE Éditions.

Develotte, Christine, Richard Kern, and Marie-Noëlle Lamy, eds. 2011. *Décrire La Conversation En Ligne : La Face à Face Distanciel*. Lyon : ENS Éditions.

Kern, Richard, and Christine Develotte. 2018. *Screens and Scenes : Multimodal Communication in Online Intercultural Encounters*. New-York ; London : Routledge. Online.

Machado, Antonio. 1917. "Campos de Castilla : Chant XXIX Proverbios y Cantarès."

Markee, Numa, and Jon Stansell. 2007. "Using Electronic Publishing as a Resource for Increasing Empirical and Interpretive Accountability in Conversation Analysis." *Annual Review of Applied Linguistics* 27 : 24–44. Online.

McQuown, Norman A, ed. 1971. *The Natural History of an Interview*. Vol. 95–98. Microfilm Collection of Manuscripts on Cultural Anthropology. Chicago : University of Chicago Library.

Merzeau, Louise. 2017. "Mémoire Partagée." In *Dictionnaire Des Biens Communs*. Paris : Presses universitaires de France. Online.

Technical issues and methodological challenges of field engineering for research

Justine Lascar
Oriane Dujour

The production and processing of corpora do not only raise methodological questions but also imply a reflection on the articulation between the work of collecting data and the requirements of the analysis. In the field of linguistic interaction analysis, this translates in particular into attention to the linguistic and multimodal details produced, mobilised, interpreted by the participants and made available by adequate recording, transcription and analysis techniques. In other words, the requirement of continuous accessibility of the relevant details of the interactions governs all the stages of the constitution and analysis of the corpora : from data collection in the field to the "manufacturing" phase, which includes audio-visual editing, transcription, alignment, annotation, up to the actual analysis phase.

These different stages in the processing of the "Digital Presences [60]" corpus are described here by considering the overlapping of numerous aspects : technical, methodological, theoretical and legal.

Recording devices

The first step in analysing interactions is the collection of situational data. Far from being a preliminary, secondary and marginal stage that could be conceived independently from the analytical objectives, data collection is an integral part of the overall process of analysis.

Collecting data is not a one-off, purely technical stage, but an undertaking that involves knowledge of the field and the

---

60. "Digital Presences" Corpus available on Ortolang.

collectors' relationships with the various actors involved, and the practical and technical dimensions of recording.

In the tradition of recording methods used in Conversation Analysis and educational sciences, we recorded the IMPEC seminars using several cameras in order to multiply the points of view. This allowed us to preserve the ecology of the situation and to have access to all the details of the interactions such as gaze, gestures, postures but also to all the online communication through screen captures taken by the different artefacts used during the seminar (Adobe Connect, Kubi and Beam telepresence robots). This research project started when we had just acquired new recording devices, in particular action cameras such as the GoPro and the Sony Action Cam, but also Kodak SP360 360° cameras. These cameras could not only be set up in places that were previously inaccessible to conventional tripod cameras, but could also take more wide-angle shots with their integrated wide-angle lens. The Digital Presences research project thus provided the opportunity to test these different devices and to reflect on their specificities and their contribution to the analysis of interactions.

The members of the "Digital Presences" group opened the doors of the seminar to us also by allowing us to test different device configurations. The Laboratory of Pedagogical and Digital Innovation Room (LipeN) is a space designed to accommodate collaborative methodological tools, and is located within the French Institute of Education (IFE) at the ENS of Lyon. The data collection had to take into account the constraints linked to the location and to the different modalities of the seminar.

The location :

    — The room has a glass wall which caused problems in the arrangement of the cameras to avoid backlighting,

— one of the walls is covered with a whiteboard which constrained where we could place the cameras,
— the furniture is modular and there are sockets on the floor. We had to take this into account for the trajectories of the Beam robot in particular.

Organisation of the seminar :

— there were several configurations : conference mode, with the speaker(s) in the centre facing the audience in a U-shape; work-group mode, with participants seated around two L-shaped tables; and once, conference mode where the speaker piloted the Beam robot with the audience facing her around an L-shaped table. For each of these configurations, we needed a specific recording device.

Video recording

Recording corpora is a material and technical operation that must be designed and carried out according to the objectives and objects of analysis. This operation aimed at recording audio/video data in order to make relevant linguistic, multimodal and situational details (gaze, gestures, movements, actions, objects, physical setting) available, and therefore analysable. We sought to record both the details that participants exploited in a situated way to produce and interpret the intelligibility of their behaviour, and those that the analysts exploited to give an account of the organisation of the interaction, based on the orientations shown by the participants.

The recordings were therefore governed by the need to take into account

— the temporal unfolding of the interaction;
— the ecology of the interaction, i.e., the way it unfolded in space;
— the framework of participation that characterised the interaction;

— the objects that were mobilised by the interactants.
To achieve these objectives, we used a variety of recording
equipment. Firstly, we used two Sony XR550 camcorders
on tripods to provide two views of the seminar :
- — the first camera was aimed at the audience –
  View 1.
- — the second was placed at the back of the room
  facing the speakers and the video content projected on the wall (Adobe Connect and presentation
  slideshow) – in the group work configuration, the
  two views were complementary – View 2.

A GoPro Hero5 camera was positioned high up a wall on a
whiteboard using a magnetic gorilla pod to record an over-
view of the room and the movements of the Beam robot –
GP view.

We set up these three views for all the seminars we recorded.
During the first session, we also tested a Kodak SP360 camera, positioned on a piece of furniture so it could be level with the interactants' faces, which interfered with the
movements of the Beam robot. Moreover, the analysis of
the 360° data is complex because it involves constructing
a point of view a posteriori. We therefore abandoned this
solution for the following sessions.

To record data involving the remote participants (different
individuals were present in each session), we had to take
into account which digital artefacts were being used and
decide how to collect their data.

For the Beam, we asked the pilot to record her screen and
a view of her environment showing her interacting in front
of her screen.

In order to record the remote use of Adobe Connect, we
also asked one of our colleagues in Aix-en-Provence to record her screen.

For Adobe Connect used in-situ in Lyon, we also collected a screen capture from a participant present in the LipeN room as well as the projection of the interface on the wall of the room using the View 1 Camera.

The Kubi stream was impossible to retrieve directly from the iPad, as the combination of the remote control and the dynamic screen capture made the connection lag; we therefore retrieved the movements of the Kubi and the image from the iPad using a Sony Action Cam placed a few centimetres away from the artefact using its built-in wide angle. To complete the picture, the screen of the computer that controlled the Kubi remotely was also recorded.

We therefore obtained between 5 and 8 different video streams for each session, – between 3 and 4 in-situ views and between 2 and 4 dynamic remote views and screen captures.

Audio recording

We used wireless Sennheiser Ew100 HF microphones connected to a Zoom H6 multitrack recorder to record the sound of the seminars. One microphone was worn by Christine one by the speaker and two others with foam insulation were placed in the room on tables close to the participants.

The multitrack recorder allows the sound to be monitored outside the room and the synchronised tracks to be recovered.

For each session, we therefore had four separate audio streams.

Video editing and export

The editing phase is also crucial in making all the elements of the interaction available and intelligible. The *Cellule Corpus Complexes*, a transversal research support team at the ICAR laboratory, uses its expertise in post-production data processing (synchronisation of the different sources, ano-nymisation, audio and video editing, etc.).

We work with Final Cut Pro X on Mac computers. After ha-ving created a library that gathered all the corpus data ser-ving as an archive, we imported all the recorded and recove-red streams. The resolution, bit rates and number of frames per second could differ depending on the source. We lis-ted and analysed them to prevent possible processing pro-blems. The first important step was to synchronise the dif-ferent audio and video streams available for each seminar (between 8 and 12 tracks). While some of the synchronisa-tion could be automated based on the soundtracks of the different streams, some was done manually.

The process went as follows : once the synchronisation was complete, we decided on a common start and end time for all the audio and video tracks ; each view was thus exported as a single file but with the same duration as all the others. The video files were exported in .mp4 format with a resolu-tion of 960 × 540, resulting in files that were not too large but of sufficient quality to provide access to the details of the interaction (the files had an average duration of one hour, and a size of about 1.2 GB each). The audio tracks were re-exported in .wav format, so as not to lose any infor-mation.

Once the files were exported, it was easy to navigate from one to the other due to their shared timing.

We then created multi-view edits using QuickTime Pro 7 software according to the team's needs.

In this way, we discussed which views to focus on and how to arrange them. In the present case, several multi-view edits were made, for example, only with the tracks filmed in-situ in Lyon

with these same tracks and the Adobe Connect screen cap-ture or only with the digital artefacts being used.

In addition to the seminar sessions, the "Digital Presences" corpus contains 17 video and audio interviews of the different team members. They were conducted after the seminars together with a questionnaire. The interviews were also transcribed.

All the audio and video tracks of the seminars, the multiscope montages as well as the interviews were made available to the whole team via the Ortolang platform (EquipEx of the TGIR Humanum). The corpus is structured and archived so as to be accessible to the members of the group in a secure manner.

Video editing choices made for a video-enhanced publication

Synopsis – collaborative work – method

The choice to publish the book in an online digital format gave the authors greater freedom to illustrate their concepts, particularly through the possibility of integrating videos into the text. The creation of the video clips aimed to add a layer of analysis through the editing processes, in addition to the raw data from the seminars.

To facilitate comprehension and avoid interrupting the flow of the article, we chose to create very short clips (less than 3 minutes) based on the model of 1 clip = 1 concept.

The clips were created in close collaboration with the authors of the book in order to preserve their intention as much as possible. Each example combines technique and analysis. The authors provided us with a list of the videos selected for study, their location in the articles and the extracts and views necessary for their creation. They then produced a written synopsis for each video clip, bringing together the various audio-visual materials and additional elements (transcription, subtitling, focus, commentary, etc.). Following this framework, we created an initial sequence with the different shots and timings requested and ensured that the different views were synchronised in order to avoid time lags.

We then repeated this editing test in the presence of a one of the authors of the chapter or by video conference when necessary[61]. The process is the result of a dialogue between the researcher and the members of the Cellule Corpus Complexes technical team about the technical proposals. Audio-visual editing tools were, in fact, used to interpret the discourse of the researcher.

The status of the video changes from raw data to a product resulting from the analysis of this data. Our aim was to reveal the researcher's point of view, i.e., to show their analysis through editing.

The video clips are treated as inseparable from the analysis presented in the articles, rather than as independent objects. Therefore, we have chosen not to contextualise the extract by detailing the subject matter in the video, since these elements are available in the associated article; this avoids a visual information overload and considerably shortens the length of the clip, so as not to be redundant with the written analysis.

Focusing attention through editing

To illustrate the authors' concepts, we used editing techniques to highlight specific elements of the corpus of data. For example, we used these different techniques to focus the reader's attention on a part of a scene:

---

61. The digital editing of the book, which began in 2019, was completed during the lockdown, so some of the clips were produced remotely.

— Progressive zoom : this allows an element to be enlarged, more or less quickly depending on the rhythm of the extract, either to completely cover the shot underneath or to have a top layer in order to show several elements at once. We used it in particular to show shots from within the artefact from which they were taken (e.g., zooming in on the view of the Kubi screen and making the enlarged picture emerge from that same screen). From an analytical point of view, zooming allows us to convey focus.

— Crop : the shot is cropped, usually after being enlarged, to remove unnecessary elements from the image. Cropping can be done either by showing the original frame and the frame change or by showing only the cropped shot.

— Blurring : when layers are superimposed, for example after progressive zooming in, blurring the lower layer makes it less visible and gives the reader less visual information. We used this technique when the focus needed to be on the Adobe Connect chat window.

— Circles : more simply, we often used turquoise circles to draw the viewer's attention to a specific element or to link a descriptive note to the element involved.

Similarly, depending on the context, we selected the audio tracks to be used and manipulated in order to focus on the exchanges, or conversely, to reduce the sound information.

Adjusting the rhythm of the video clips

We paced the clips so that they remained short, and so the reader was not cut off from the text for too long.

In general, we mainly used cuts to change shots but, in some cases, we used the zoom to indicate which interface the new shot came from. When it was important to show several views simultaneously (for example, to show the same action from two different angles), we used a split screen, i.e., dividing the screen into two or more parts, each filled by a different shot.

In cases where the analysis involved a long extract or even a complete session, we used two procedures :

— Acceleration : an 8-fold or more increase in the speed of the video.

— A fade to black between two shots : the first shot darkens until the screen is completely black and then the second shot gradually appears to indicate a time jump.

Conveying a clear analysis

The clarity of the situations depended in particular on a visual contextualisation of the superimposed shots. This was achieved by the technique, mentioned above, of zooming in from the artefact, but also by applying filters to the shots. For example, in order to indicate the sequences that were accelerated, we applied a visual effect (Frame in Final Cut Pro) that streaked the image with thin green stripes, and added a double animated arrow, similar to the Fast Forward symbol on VCRs.

As another example, for the shots from one of the recording cameras, we used the *cam recorder* filter, which applies a frame and a symbol indicating the current recording.

In order to clarify certain passages in the video or to convey a specific point of the researcher's analysis, we also used text boxes :

— Text in white Courier font on a dark grey band : used for transcriptions of spoken words when these are important for the analysis.

— Text in black Comfortaa font on a turquoise band : used to describe or contextualise an action, and to propose an analysis.
— Text in black Comfortaa font in a turquoise bubble : used for messages posted in the chat window. The shape and animation of the bubble are reminiscent of instant messengers.

It was often difficult to find a good compromise between the clarity and briefness of the textual explanations, which had to be easy to read and avoid disrupting attention too much when viewing the clip. The authors chose the sentences to use in the edited video, and the rewordings were chosen together with the technical team.

Export and archiving

A major issue was to find a secure, permanent storage place that would allow the videos to be broadcasted on the publisher's website. We chose to host them on the ATV (Archiving and Transcoding Video) platform created and managed by the ENS, where we archived the clips in .mp4 format after indexing them. ATV also allows users to upload enriched videos, for example, with a subtitle file.

Collaborating with the different authors of this book from various disciplinary fields has been a truly enriching experience. The members of the Cellule Corpus Complexes were part and parcel of the research team throughout the phases of the project, from data collection to the publication of the book. Our thoughts and experiences nourished each other. This five-year collaborative project has allowed us to explore, test and experiment with our working methods, and to enrich them with different disciplinary perspectives, always with mutual benevolence.

Acknowledgements

Christine Develotte

This research was, more than any other, a team effort. Beyond the work of the sole authors, various people were involved more or less directly, and we would like to extend our deepest gratitude to them.

To the speakers who agreed for their picture to be used in our study. First of all, our first guests, Axel Guïoux (Université Lyon 2) and Évelyne Lasserre (Université Lyon 1), who kindly accepted to participate in our seminar to present their work [62]. Then, Susan Herring (Indiana University, USA), an eminent specialist in the field of screen-based communication, who presented her work on robots [63]. We wish to thank you sincerely for feeding into our reflection on screen-based interactions in the context of our polyartefacted doctoral seminar.

To our colleagues who participated more or less regularly in our seminars, who were also filmed and are part of our data collection : Jacques Cosnier (Université Lyon 2), Françoise Poyet (Université Lyon 1) and Liping Zhang (Hangzhou University, China). To Yigong Guo, a PhD student at the ICAR laboratory, who was a regular participant in these seminars, and Prisca Fenoglio, a PhD student at Paris 8 University, who also participated briefly in a videoconference during the first session. We would like to express our appreciation to these colleagues for allowing us to use their image for research purposes.

To our colleagues from the technical team of the ICAR laboratory who were involved in the different stages of our work, as shown in the appendix "Technical issues and methodological challenges of field engineering for research". We are deeply indebted to the team led by Justine Lascar,

---

62. Conference "Mobilis Immobile - La présence au-delà de l'empêchement".

63. Conference "Discourse Pragmatics of Robot Mediated Communication".

with the ad hoc collaboration of Laurie Boyer, Julien Gachet, and Luca and Gerry Niccolaï. This past year, Oriane Dujour's work on the digital publication process saved us some precious time. The ease with which she got on board with the project, her interest in computerised documentation, and her talent as an illustrator helped us greatly.

We are also grateful to the Education team of the French Institute of Education (Ifé), who allowed us to use their multifunctional room for the seminar in Lyon. We also used the Beam robot, which was lent to us by Ifé, and we therefore wish to thank this institution.

Thanks should also go to Gilles Pouchoulin for welcoming us and for his availability to answer our questions during our first steps on the Ortolang platform, and for his careful follow-up of our project.

We are deeply indebted to the Montreal team : first of all, for taking an immediate interest in our editorial project and for proposing a collaboration with Les Ateliers de [sens public]. Secondly, for accepting to come to Lyon to hold training sessions on the text editor Stylo, and finally, for their proofreading work and their support with matters of digital publishing. Our warmest thanks go to Hélène Beauchef, Servanne Monjour, Nicolas Sauret and Marcello Vitali Rosati.

Finally, this research has benefited from funding from the Labex Aslan, the ICAR laboratory, the Canada Research Chair on Digital Textualities and the Interuniversity Research Centre on Digital Humanities.

This book was produced using LaTeX through the [sens public] workflow. The tex document was generated with pandoc from markdown, bibtex and yaml source files, composed in Stylo text editor.

www.ingramcontent.com/pod-product-compliance
Lightning Source LLC
Chambersburg PA
CBHW071337290326
41933CB00039B/1319